SOUL RECOVERY
AND
EXTRACTION

Ai Gvhdi Waya

Blue Turtle Publishing
P.O. Box 2513
Cottonwood, AZ 86326

Copyright 1992 by Ai Gvhdi Waya
Copyright 1993 by Ai Gvhdi Waya, ISBN: 0-9634662-3-2
2nd Edition, August, 1993

Third edition, 1998

SOUL RECOVERY

AND

EXTRACTION

by
AI GVHDI WAYA

DEDICATED TO:

Our Spirit Guides and Pte Hey Chola Wakan Wi,
White Buffalo Calf Woman

TABLE OF CONTENTS

INTRODUCTION

SOUL RECOVERY is about regaining the fragments of one's soul energy that have been trapped, lost or stolen either by another person or through a traumatic incident that has occurred in one's life. Taking back control of your life is at the heart of this shamanistic healing method.

The most pervasive sense of soul loss is an impression that something in our life is missing. Or, we just do not feel quite together like we used to. There is a suspicion of imbalance, or being out of sync with ourselves, and yet, we cannot explain adequately as to why we feel this way.

Shamanism, in the simplest of definitions, is the ability of an individual to move into an altered state and travel the inner dimensions of what we call nonphysical reality. This technique is as old as humans have been here on earth. It is practiced around the world, and in the last decade, has been reintroduced to Western civilization — although among indigenous cultures, continues to be practiced as a healing tool without interruption.

EXTRACTION is another tool within the shamanistic tradition that dissolves "blocks" from our bodies or the aura of electromagnetic energy that surrounds each of us. These blocks can affect us physically, as well as mentally, emotionally or spiritually, and with a shaman's expertise, can be removed.

Shamanism, soul recovery and extraction can help an individual achieve a return to health. So many physical diseases have their roots or beginning in our soul, which eventually manifests into a specific form of disease within our physical body. Shamanism can remove the root cause that is found in the soul of a person and assist true healing on all levels of that individual.

This book is about my own odyssey into shamanism, and how it has helped those who have come for healing of their soul. You somehow feel you are not all you used to be — it could be true. You might be missing energy or power that has left you with a weakened or "vacant" feeling. This book will open up a wealth of further possibilities to be explored in your quest for wellness — on all levels.

Why is shamanism, specifically, the real of journeying to retrieve pieces and extraction, becoming so popular? This healing tool is as old as man and womankind, and yet has remained undetected by mainstream society in most cultures. I feel that with all the earth changes and the spiritual acceleration that is taking place, shamanic journeying is a must. Why? Because those of us who expect to grow and accelerate with the increased frequency tempo all need our pieces back in order to "keep up" with the dramatic and powerful shifts.

Furthermore, without our pieces we are out of balance and out of harmony with ourselves. Mother Earth is out of balance, and she is now doing a great deal to shift and come back to her own center. This includes the many earthquakes, floods, the strange shifting weather patterns, plagues and general "shake up" that will continue for at least another 20 years. Those who are in harmony with themselves have automatic protection. One does not get sick if one is in balance within themselves.

Five years ago the Harmonic Convergence took place. For the next nine-year cycle, according to Mayan prophecy, each year after the initial "burst" of energy or stepping up of frequency vibration for the planet, another burst of energy/vibration would be released, usually in either June or July of each successive year. We are five years into this acceleration. It is literally vibrating people apart on all levels of themselves. Job losses, divorces, murders, the appalling rape of women in record numbers and the abuse of children are indications of the breaking down and dissolving that this acceleration is causing to those who have missing pieces. The intensity becomes more powerful with each year, so that the next four years, 1993 through 1997, are going to be even more catalytic. You can liken each release to an earthquake moving up one point higher on the Richter Scale with each occurrence.

Have your pieces returned to you so that you can be in

the Cosmic flow of this shift, and your life will even out? You will, with Soul Recovery and Extraction, then be able to meet the forthcoming challenges with balance and harmony. That is why soul recovery and extraction is surfacing — it is a healing tool, an answer to surviving with harmony during this time of chaos in our lives.

CHAPTER 1

WHAT IS SOUL LOSS AND SOUL RECOVERY?

SOUL LOSS:

Soul loss is about losing or giving away part of our energy, who we are, to another person or situation. This energy is seen as "soul" to some, and to others, a facet of our personality. The labels are meaningless, because something is lost that was once yours. Soul loss is usually undetected at first, but over time, the individual who has suffered the loss feels it in many ways that will be covered later in this book. There are several ways to lose a piece of yourself:

Stealing: In a psychological sense, a codependent person is constantly giving away her/his energy, time, focus and self. A person who has a victim's mentality (usually abused women, men or children) will also unconsciously give away pieces of themselves to those who are more than willing to take them. People who feel they are unlovable, suffer from low self-esteem or have shame issues, give pieces of themselves away. Often the "taker" is the other spouse, a child, relative, friend or sometimes a co-worker.

Accidents: In a severe accident, there is always shock and trauma. How you perceive the accident will determine whether or not a piece is split off during the traumatic incident. An accident where there is surgery afterward, a coma or extended length of unconsciousness, should always be suspect.

Emotional Reasons: This is the main arena of loss for all of us. These involve the death of a loved one, child or otherwise; the death of a beloved pet that was your entire

1

world; a move from one location to another; a move from one country to another; sexual molestation or rape; abuse by a parent; abandonment issues (orphans, adopted children, foster home children) and suppression of minority groups (women, African Americans, Native Americans, Hispanics, etc.).

Any time a person becomes a victim, there can be a loss of a fragment of the self that becomes trapped in the emotional trauma. That means that all victims play an unconscious, psychological game with their perpetrator. If the victim can get out of that "dance", then the piece given to the perpetrator returns to the victim. If not, the "dance" between them continues and the victim has lost much more than s/he realizes.

When a woman is continuously told or given messages from our male-ruled society that she is second best, not as important, not as smart or resourceful, not as intelligent nor as able, huge energy chunks of a female's soul/personality split off. The result is codependence. Codependence occurs when one party (regardless of gender) gives and gives — not knowing when to stop giving. Consequently, the person becomes exhausted, embittered and angry towards the "taker". Codependent people do not know how to set up healthy boundaries so there can be a balance between giving and taking. They do not know how to say *no* to anyone or any situation because they also are afraid of not being liked or rejected. They, therefore, become depleted of more than just physical energy; they start giving pieces of themselves away, too.

Mentally, our attitudes can either create a prison for us, or set us free. Our early environments and our parents' attitudes and beliefs all contribute to making us whole, or splitting us apart as individuals.

A good example of mental entrapment is when we feel overly responsible for others. This is found more often in women than in men, and is an aspect of codependent behavior. Women are taught to give, give, give without any thought of giving back to themselves. This sets in motion not only mental, but emotional burnout as well. The result is a loss of pieces of a woman's soul to those who continually take, take, take from her give, give, give position.

Further, addictions are often at the root of soul loss. It could be addiction to love, sex, drugs, gambling, codependence, alcohol or the tendency to repeat the same mistake over and over again. All are signs of soul loss.

Spiritually, one can lose a soul piece by giving power away to someone/something else. Mindless belief in anything courts disaster when you underestimate the power of the individual involved. Spiritual "brainwashing" often takes a piece of a person's soul. Look at the religions known to practice a mindless "believe in me or else" sort of belief.

Native Americans believe that following your own inner guidance is the best way to learn and to respect your unique individuality. To surrender this to anything or anyone is unthinkable.

DO I NEED SOUL RECOVERY?

There are certain "red flags" that may show that a person has lost major pieces of their soul and need a shaman (I'm using this term to denote either female or male who practices this art/skill/talent) to journey for them, locate the missing pieces and bring them back. Here are some warning signals that you might need soul recovery:

1. **Schizophrenia** is a condition where a large number of pieces are missing — usually due to childhood emotional trauma.

2. **Multiple Personality Disorder (MPD)** (the Three Faces of Eve). Individuals with this disorder suffered through great emotional/mental trauma during baby/childhood and developed compartmentalized personalities to deal with the ongoing traumas.

3. **Depression** of any kind that is diagnosed as chronic or ongoing. When we lose enough pieces, we become depressed — grieving for our missing pieces. This also includes manic depression.

4. **Inability to ground oneself.** This is someone who

is constantly daydreaming, shows a lack of interest in daily life and wants to escape by watching TV, drinking alcohol, consuming drugs, "checking out" or is considered a "space cadet". This person usually runs around frantically, is completely disorganized and has little self discipline. These ungrounded people have literally, in the astral sense, pulled up and out of their physical bodies. This is usually from the knees upward, because it is simply too painful for them to be 100% grounded and connected to reality. They also "lift off" because there are parts missing, and they feel terribly vulnerable. Therefore, they try to escape by leaving their body.

5. **Detachment** or feeling as if you are standing outside yourself and seeing the world pass by without being connected to it. This may be accompanied by sociopathic behavior. The person exhibits no morals, values or principles. In fact, there is no sense of anyone else existing except themselves and what they want out of life. Emotions will be numb, and sometimes there is physical numbness somewhere in the body. There may also be a sense of helplessness, giving up or feeling immune to human or animal suffering in general.

6. **Blocks of memory loss.** Anytime you cannot remember a certain age of your life, soul loss has occurred. The piece that has that memory is no longer there for you to recall what happened. Usually, huge blocks of memory (say, from age 6 to 12) show that a trauma occurred, soul loss followed, and memory loss replaced it.

7. **Chronic illness** from the time you were born through age ten to twelve years old. Soul loss can occur to the baby during pregnancy, during labor/birth and shortly after birth. If this happens, the baby has a long, chronic history of always catching every cold, flu and childhood disease — and then some. For example, I was chronically ill from the time I was born until, at two years old, I had to have my tonsils removed — an unheard of surgery in 1948 — and I almost died. I then continued to contract every cold and flu until I was five years old, and then contracted scarlet

fever. At age six, I had rheumatic fever, which put a hole in my heart. At age eleven I had mononucleosis, and at age twelve, I had hepatitis. (At a much later age, the missing pieces were returned to me.)

If you had a major illness between birth and twelve years old, this can be indicative of soul loss, too.

8. **Addiction** of any kind, including drugs, alcohol, codependency, food (anorexia as well as bulimia), sex (sexual molester, rapist), love, gambling, etc. Or, repetition of same mistake over and over again. For example: choosing to continue marrying abusive men, or creating difficult work situations over and over again.

9. **Unable to release** a divorce, the death of a loved one or the death of a pet. Your life revolves around the past and it becomes an obsession that you cannot seem to release, stop thinking about or stop feeling about.

10. **Mentally asking: why am I here?** A sense of emptiness, of not connecting or being connected as you know instinctively that you should be. A sense of knowing you are not whole, but being unable to express it that way.

11. **Continual cycles of colds or flu** — no matter how many antibiotics you have taken, and at any age. Or, contracting immune system diseases, such as arthritis, cancer, AIDs. If you are easily stressed, there could be soul loss. When stress reaches the immune system, it buckles because the missing piece is not there to support it.

12. **A vague feeling of impending doom** often appears when many pieces are lost. The individual begins to feel terribly vulnerable and may unconsciously sense that something is missing.

13. **Obesity and unexplained/explained weight** gain is a normal pattern for sexually molested and/or raped women. The woman will unconsciously eat more food to provide a physical barrier of fat between herself and the outside world of men. She makes herself unattractive to avoid being attacked again. The sexual molester/rapist has a large part of her soul still in his possession, even long after the violent deed has been done.

14. **Abuse/violence** of any kind against a child or adult most always involves soul loss. The abuser, even if now dead, has a piece of that person.

15. **Loss of self-esteem**, the feeling of shame and lack of confidence, are all signals of major soul loss. Women often suffer from this because they are gender-suppressed in our society.

16. EXPRESSIONS USED BY THOSE WHO HAVE SOUL LOSS:

- *I just don't feel whole.*
- *I know s/he has a piece of me!*
- *I feel as if there's a gaping hole here, in me.*
- *I just feel lost, as if I have no direction, no goals.*
- *I can't sleep well at night.*
- *S/he stole a part of me.*
- *S/he still has a strangle hold on me.*
- *I feel as if s/he's still got me even though s/he's dead & buried.*
- *I'm tired all the time; I just don't have any pep or energy.*
- *I feel as if I'm an extremist; I can't do anything middle-of-the-road. I have to go to extremes.*
- *S/he hates me.*
- *I have dreams about this person; it's as if they are haunting me.*
- *I feel like I'm a slave to that person.*
- *I feel out of kilter, out of balance, but don't know why!*
- *I feel like a cripple, but I shouldn't!*
- *Life is just one gray color to me.*
- *My senses feel dead; I don't feel any joy or sadness.*
- *I can't cry — I haven't for years.*
- *I feel as if s/he's controlling me, and I don't have the strength to say no to them.*
- *I feel as if I'm being torn apart by all of them.*
- *I feel like a puppet just waiting for my family to jerk my strings.*

WHY DOES SOUL LOSS OCCUR?

In our imperfect world of imperfect people, there is such a thing as a soul thief. This is an individual who (usually) unconsciously steals a piece of a person's soul because of a deep psychological/emotional need. To feel whole themselves, they steal from others. If soul thieving is done consciously, we say the thief is a sorcerer. This is, fortunately, a rarity.

Most often we know a piece is missing when we are with a person who makes us feel suddenly very tired, exhausted or as if our own vital force plug had been pulled out. This is the world of the psychic vampire, a soul thief who has put his "gasoline pump" into your aura and begun sucking you dry. In fact, this individual can take a piece of the victim and drain energy for decades without either thief or victim consciously aware of what is going on.

Sometimes a person will take a piece of another person to protect her. Most soul theft is done unconsciously. The person taking the piece does not realize they are doing it, or the subsequent damage that soul loss can inflict on the victim.

Sometimes we unconsciously give a piece of ourselves away. This is called codependency — a rampant problem nowadays.

Parents can take a piece of their children. The child then becomes grievously ill or catches cycles of colds/flu for years on end. Usually the thief is a hardworking mother. She's exhausted by the brutal demands upon her time both job-wise and home-wise, is giving too much of herself to her husband and critically needs enough energy to keep on going. So, she steals from her child.

A father who lusts after his daughter (even if it is just a thought) will take a piece of her soul and keep it. As she moves through puberty and into adulthood, sexuality problems will arise. A woman who needs security may cling to her spouse and take a piece of him — even to the grave and beyond.

Everyone has experienced soul loss and has probably taken soul fragments from another person — and it's usually a loved one, be it the spouse, a relative or a child. When soul loss becomes major, then a bevy of problems will begin to occur, as noted above.

Does everyone need soul recovery? Unequivocally, yes! Getting back your pieces can be accomplished in different ways. For instance, people who do not believe in shamanism may go to a therapist and spend years getting a "breakthrough", which is when a piece is retrieved by the person themselves. There are as many ways to get back one's pieces as there are healing techniques. What counts is this: whatever form of healing you believe in will be the one that is "right" for you to get your pieces back. You do not necessarily need the shamanistic method to accomplish this — although I will say that it will cut off years of personal "searching" and "working" to get a piece back, and infinitely less expensive from a financial standpoint.

HOW IS SOUL RECOVERY ACCOMPLISHED?

A person can be specially trained to accomplish soul recovery. This individual is seen as a shamanic facilitator, one who can move into an altered state of consciousness and journey to the other worlds or dimensions where these pieces are "stuck" or held by a living or deceased person. More discussion about this will appear later.

To perform soul recovery, there is a specific ceremony that involves a shaman and client, drum and a rattle, and perhaps a song. The details of how a shaman journeys to find these missing soul pieces and how they recover the soul are closely guarded secrets.

Usually, a client will come to my medicine room where I not only meditate, but utilize the area for healings. Since I am Cherokee Metis (part Cherokee), my medicine room contains a buffalo robe on the floor. I always tell my client before I journey what s/he can expect because I want the person to trust and to be relaxed, not on edge or curious.

We both take off our shoes and any jewelry (with the

exception of a wedding ring), and the client lies down on their back on the robe. There is a pillow for under their head and a blanket in case they would like to cover up, as some people get cold during the process.

My drumming assistant, my mother Ruth, sits at our feet as I lay down next to the client. She will do the drumming that places me in the altered state for the journey. I place my left hand over the client's right hand and close my eyes.

How long does journeying take? It all depends upon the shaman. I know one woman who takes up to one hour to make a journey on a client's behalf. Others can do the same in ten minutes. Time is not an indicator of success.

How many pieces are brought back? That is entirely dependent upon my chief guide who makes that decision. I have brought back as few as two, and as many as nine pieces. In my experience with people I draw to me, an average of three pieces are returned on the first journey.

Then, three months after the first journey and after the pieces have been "integrated" and absorbed back into the person's soul or personality, I will journey again on behalf of the client and ask if there are any more pieces to retrieve. Usually there are more pieces to be returned.

The most traumatized pieces may return with the last journey for the client. It's almost as if the guides realize that the client must have a slow, natural adjustment period to pieces being brought back. That is why they do not bring back the most important nor most deeply traumatized pieces on that first journey.

Most adults require three journeys, three months apart — much like a nine-month pregnancy, if one wants to look at it in a rebirthing or symbolic sense.

Children usually require only one if they are babies, or two at the most until age twelve. This can vary, depending upon the type of trauma they have experienced and how often.

Once I leave on the journey, I am taken to the Dark, Real and Light Worlds to be shown where these pieces are "stuck" or stolen or held by an individual. I do not necessarily traverse all three dimensions; sometimes I go only to the Dark and Real Worlds for a client.

Different shamanic facilitators see different things on a journey. For instance, I always see the soul piece as a symbol. Ardella Hecht, an associate, receives feelings and sometimes a vision. Other facilitators may hear or see a word, message or a full sentence. Every shaman receives whatever they need for their client in a form that is revealed by the spirit guides. There is no one way or right way to receive these messages. They may come in an impression, a word, a symbol, a vision or a voice.

LONG DISTANCE JOURNEYING

Our facilitators have been trained to journey, literally, around the world for their client. What this means, is that the client does not have to travel to see the facilitator in person to have Soul Recovery and Extraction (from here on, to be referred to as SR/E) performed. Not all shamans can journey long distance to perform an SR/E, and most, instead, see the client in person. Long distance journeying is a very unique and rare talent among shamans of the world. By being able to do long distance journeying on behalf of the client, this saves the client airline and lodging expenses.

It does not matter whether our facilitators see you physically, in person, or if they see you and perform SR/E on you long distance. The result is the same, and there is no difference regardless of which technique is employed by the facilitator.

There is no linear time or distance involved in the other dimensions that shamans travel within. Therefore, it is easy for our facilitators to literally "pop in" and perform SR/E for a client. For further information and understanding of this phenomena, I suggest you read *The Holographic Universe* by Michael Talbot.

CASE HISTORY EXAMPLE: (Name changed per client's wish.) Cindy is in her mid-thirties and came to me for soul recovery. The first place my guides sent me, I found myself covered with red blood. It was everywhere! I was drenched in it, flying through it, unable to see anything but a wall of red color. Finally, I asked my hawk to take me above the color to see what was going on. There was a huge blob of red blood floating in the Dark World. I captured it with my net and took it back to my client.

I was then returned to the Dark World once again, to a swamp. Here I saw a man with two heads: one was human, the other a slavering wolf, his teeth bared and foaming at the mouth. He had a red and yellow ball of light that belonged to Cindy. As I looked down at this hideous man, I saw a shackle and chain around his leg that extended to Cindy's leg. I asked him for the balls of light, which he refused to give me. So, I traded him a heart-shaped rose quartz stone for them. When I began to saw the chain in two, he began to howl and became very agitated with me. I realized that the chain symbolically bound her with this man, and I quickly cut it in half and freed Cindy.

I was then sent to the Light World and was taken to a hunched-over, petite, thin-looking old woman with steel gray hair gathered in a tight bun at the nape of her neck. Her features were sharp looking and she was wearing an apron over a plain cotton print dress that hung to her ankles. Smiling, she came forward and greeted me. She handed me a gold key and said to give this back to Cindy. She told me she was the woman's grandmother, and that the key would help her unlock things she needed to know about herself. The grandmother said she had been waiting a long time to give her granddaughter this gift.

Next, I was taken to the Real World to Cindy's mother. The mother handed me a lavender-colored paper heart with white lace glued around the edges of it. The heart reminded me of something a first or second grader would have made on Valentine's Day.

When I returned with the pieces, I got up on my knees and "blew" the pieces back into Cindy's heart chakra, sat her up and blew the pieces back into her crown chakra at the top of her head. I then laid my client back down, and with my spider rattle, I shook it in a clockwise motion four times around her entire body to seal her up.

Cindy then sat up with my help and I welcomed her home. The drumming stopped. I told Cindy what I had seen and what had been given to me. Cindy said the man in the swamp was her father — that he was like a Jekyll and Hyde personality. He was an alcoholic and had committed suicide. For me, this explained why the father was in the swamp in the Dark World. I would frequently come to the swamp for a soul who had committed suicide or died within the grip of some kind of addiction. Sometimes, the soul preferred the Dark World instead of traversing the Real World after death.

The red and yellow lights he had of Cindy's, I felt, was the energy he had stolen from her solar plexus, which is yellow in color, and the red is the root chakra. I felt he had sexually molested her as a youngster; hence, the stealing of the root chakra sexual energy. Because he was an alcoholic, he played havoc on her emotions, which are kept in the solar plexus region. I felt the chain was self-explanatory — he still had a "hold" over her even in death. I also felt that she might possibly feel guilty over his death, perhaps taking the blame, or she had not begun to work through the chaos of emotions that he had unleashed within her because of his addiction.

Cindy told me that she had felt her femininity had been at stake, that she had cystic fibroids in her breasts, and at 30 had already had a hysterectomy! These types of illnesses in the reproductive region of a woman's body always point a finger toward sexual molestation as a baby or child, rape as an adult and may or may not be recalled by the woman. However, Cindy did not have any recall about this, but she did have a spotty memory, with no recall until she was about ten years old. I invited her to read *The Courage to Heal* by Ellen Bass (Harper & Row), a book about survivors of sexual molestation and rape, to see if she saw her own patterns of behavior in it. I knew that with the pieces being brought back from her father, that within three months she would start recalling the molestation.   With the piece returning the memory also comes back.

The blob of blood, I felt, was indicative of one of several things: it could have been a rough labor where her mother bled profusely during the birthing of Cindy; or it could have symbolized her father's suicide; or her own female menses blood, her femininity being stolen by her father. Cindy said the labor/birth was not bad, so that was discounted. I told her that sooner or later she would know what that blob of blood meant to her personally.

A shaman may or may not be able to interpret the symbols returned to the client. Usually, I let my clients tell me what they feel or think about the symbol. If they do not know (50% of the time they won't know), then I will share suggestions based upon my experience of journeying.

The gift that her grandmother gave Cindy was self-explanatory, and I bet the grandmother knew about the father sexually molesting Cindy as a baby/child. A key means to open up something to view it. I did not tell Cindy this at the time.

The lavender paper heart was symbolic that her mother had a piece of Cindy's heart, and that she had taken this piece when Cindy was in the first grade.   Interestingly, Cindy recalled that she had made just such a paper heart for her mother at that age — same color and design.

On this first journey for Cindy, she had gotten two pieces back from her father, a piece from her mother, a piece of her femininity which was trapped in time (the red blob of blood) and a gift of a key from her grandmother.

One of the first things I look for after I have blown soul pieces back into the client is: how do their eyes look? If the ceremony has worked, the client's eyes are always full of life and sparkling afterward.

It is common that most clients do not feel anything after the pieces are blown back into them. A few will feel the pieces return, sit up afterward and cry, or feel euphoric emotion. I always take my time with a client, because I am never sure how they will be feeling. Some burst into tears; some sit there with the biggest grin in the world across their face; others feel nothing. All of these sensations are normal.

I always warn a client that usually 12 to 72 hours after a soul recovery journey, they will feel emotionally up and down — much like a roller coaster of feelings. Why? Because the pieces retrieved flew off during a trauma; and they return in the same condition — in crisis. The morning after the journey, most people may feel lighter, happier, see the world through different eyes, feel as if a load has been taken off their shoulders, a boundless joy or some other very sharp, well-defined emotion.

Other things can happen. Depending upon how large a piece was returned, and the intensity of the trauma it comes back in, some clients may feel plunged into depression, crying jags or vomiting (usually once or twice only) several weeks after the recovery. They may have vivid dreams, sudden and unexpected recall from the past, severe emotional highs and lows. Eventually, all these things disappear — usually within three weeks of the recovery. Although, I know of one client who spent three months crying and grieving for a piece that had returned. Afterward, she was fine.

CAN YOU LOSE PIECES BROUGHT BACK?

Yes, you can. This happens with my clients about five percent of the time. A client, for whatever reason, may unconsciously reject a piece or pieces. That piece then returns to where it was before. The reason for the rejection can be that the client was not prepared for the emotional storm that follows with the return of the piece and did not have proper counseling, help or guidance in place to help deal with the integration of this piece.

Or, the client just simply does not have the strength to deal with the piece, or the information it has brought back. For example: if the piece is about sexual molestation, the client may not subconsciously be prepared to accept the truth that her father did this to her. Instead of embracing the truth, the client rejects the piece subconsciously, and the piece splits off again and returns to where it was stuck before.

Sometimes, the client is in such emotional turmoil and the pain is so great, a piece will leave. It is not necessarily one that was returned. Because the client is overwhelmed by the return of a piece, s/he cannot contain all the pieces, and loses one or more.

When this happens, the client almost invariably knows when the piece leaves — they will consciously feel as if something is missing. The client should call the facilitator and ask them to journey to validate this. A journey will be made at your request to see what has happened.

When the facilitator has spoken to the piece that has left, they will be given instructions by their chief guide. In some cases, the piece is brought back with the suggestion of therapy to commence immediately afterward. In some cases, the piece is left behind for three months while the client integrates the other pieces, and it will be brought back at a later date.

The client should not feel guilty, bad or ashamed if a newly acquired piece splits off and leaves. It rarely happens because our chief guide knows just how much the client can handle, and instructs the facilitator on how many pieces, and which pieces to retrieve. Still, healing is a free-will choice on the part of the client, and if they don't want a particular piece back just yet, we have to honor that decision.

A facilitator never makes the decision to find a certain piece. For instance, a client might say: I was raped and I want that piece back from the rapist. The shaman journeys and speaks with their chief guide to get permission. Sometimes we get permission, and the guide will take us to that piece. At other times, we do not receive permission, and we do not get the piece for the client. If we do not receive permission, the facilitator will always ask the chief guide for an explanation. Usually, I will bring a message back to the person as to why the piece cannot be brought back at this time.

The good news is: all the pieces a person has missing can eventually be returned. For an adult, it is almost a year-long process. For a child, it's usually a much shorter process. And, even better news: control of our life is in our hands once more! We can consciously elect to keep these pieces or allow them to leave us. We control our own healing process at a speed that is correct for us.

ARE THERE ANY PHYSICAL REACTIONS TO SOUL RECOVERY?

Yes, there can be. As mentioned earlier, one of the physical symptoms some clients experience is vomiting. Actually, they are purging suppressed feelings from their solar plexus (stomach) region, just above the navel. From the shaman's standpoint, this vomiting is a very good sign that the piece will stay and integrate.

Recently, Paula (not her real name) called me to tell me that she had vomited twice — but the funny thing was she did not have any signs or symptoms that she had the flu. Paula was being taken care of by Mary Buckner, my associate. I remembered talking to Mary about Paula's case a week before. Mary had left my phone number case of an emergency, since she was traveling and lecturing in several other states for a two-week period of time.

Paula had soul recovery performed by Mary approximately a month earlier. Last week, Paula had felt a piece leave her. Mary journeyed, and sure enough, the piece had left Paula. So, the piece agreed to come back to Paula and try to integrate again. This time, Paula devoted some serious time to "talk" with the piece, about her relationship to it during meditation every day. The piece began to integrate and a week later, the vomiting bouts occurred.

I told Paula this was an excellent sign, congratulated her on her hard, focused work on sincerely loving this piece and letting it know she truly wanted it to stay. I told her to call Mary and inform her of the results when she returned from her road trip.

Vomiting does not last long — perhaps once. In very

rare cases, a client might vomit two or three times in a twenty-four hour period. If it goes any longer than that, the client should call the facilitator, and a journey should be undertaken to see what's going on.

There are many physical changes that take place when pieces begin to return. One of them is loss of weight (if you're overweight)! Very frequently women who have been sexually molested (and have no recall of it) put on added weight around their hips and abdominal area (the reproductive organs), plus, in the breast region.

In one case that was handled by Patty Running, Lakota shaman and associate, she journeyed for a woman who lost ten to fifteen pounds of water weight after an extraction! It also enabled the woman to quit taking diuretics. Other weight gains involving fat cells will come off more slowly; and, it will occur as the pieces come back, over a period of time.

A person who has had soul repair has a vibrant, healthy and alive look in their eyes — they sparkle and dance. Their skin tone may also improve. Probably the most pronounced physical sensation is a return of energy. A person does not tire as easily, is not always exhausted, can become a human dynamo of sorts, needs less sleep or will have better/deeper sleep, and can develop a bounce to their step, a squaring of their shoulders and a lifting of their chin.

Let me share with you a journey I took on behalf of my Grandmother, Inez, in 1991; she was 94 at the time. To my amazement, my chief guide wanted nine pieces brought back to her! This was the most pieces I have ever returned. I was concerned, but went ahead with the journey.

An hour after the pieces were brought back, my Grandmother suffered heart pains and shortness of breath. She called us over to her house, which was about three hundred free away from my mother's home and my own. We went rushing over there to find her feeling very faint, lightheaded and gasping for breath. Fortunately, I realized what had happened, and I had brought along a homeopathic remedy to help her. She has had a long history of heart problems — angina, to be specific — so I had dealt with these cyclic attacks for years. One could say that the angina attack had nothing to do with the soul recovery because of her fifty-year history of them. But I knew from many years of soul recovery that there almost always is some kind of physical reaction to the returning pieces.

As I gave her the remedy, took her blood pressure and placed my arm around her to soothe her, I knew in my heart that the nine returning pieces had "taken". We cured her angina attack — thanks to the homeopathic remedy.

That was three years ago. My Grandmother has changed markedly — for the better — and it's a joy and pleasure to see her whole once again. That one physical reaction to so many pieces being brought back taught me a lesson — to be on the lookout for such physical responses if a client has a history of some chronic disease. My guide had decided nine pieces was acceptable, and I followed that decision. As a shaman, I do not have the choice to personally decide that it should be less or more — to do so is to invite that client's karma on myself, and I am not going to knowingly do that.

EXTRACTION:
ANOTHER ASPECT OF SOUL RECOVERY

What is extraction? It sounds as if it's a dentist's expression, doesn't it? In a sense, it is. The dentist uses a drill to extract decay out of a tooth. In the same sense, a shaman can also extract decay out of a client's aura. My own experience with extraction is covered in chapter three. Extraction means removing "block" or thought form from an individual's aura or from their physical body. If you are aware of the Philippine faith healers, then you have a good idea of what a shaman does — the same thing. They have achieved world-wide fame for this form of shamanism.

For example, let's say someone gets very angry at you and you feel as if they are shooting daggers at you. When a person gets angry enough, they can unconsciously create a thought form of energy in the other dimensions that surround us, and then fling that dagger of anger at you. The dagger thought form lodges in one or more of your auric fields (there are nine of them). This dagger, if it stays, will begin to bleed off energy from that field. If it stays there long enough, depending upon where it was aimed — let's say, the stomach — then the client may experience digestive upset, or at the worst, ulcers or trouble in that region of the body.

A person's chakras are also vulnerable to trauma. If the trauma is bad enough, it can "blow" a chakra — meaning that some or all the petals or propellers that make it move round and round to pull in prana or energy, are destroyed, bent or clogged with debris.

We have chakras both on the front and back of our auric body. Most metaphysicians know this, but many do not. Our throat chakra extends through our neck so that we have a chakra opening at the throat and in the center rear of the neck.

If any rear chakra(s) is shut down or clogged, this has to do with the person's "will". If any front chakra(s) is shut down or clogged, this deals with a person's "emotions". A shaman can perform extraction before or after soul recovery, depending on what the chief guide wants for the person. Or, extraction may be performed months after a soul recovery. Sometimes, with the returning of a piece, the extraction is not necessary because that area of the body repairs itself.

Extraction, as I was taught, and teach my students, is a secondary consideration to the health and wellness of my client. Soul recovery comes first.

For instance, if someone comes to me for homeopathic treatment, I insist that they have soul recovery done first. I have them call me a month later to "report in". After talking with the client, I will know whether or not they still need homeopathic treatment.

In some cases, the people need absolutely no homeopathic consideration! As the pieces integrate, the person's health improves.

HOW DOES A SHAMAN PERFORM EXTRACTION?

Each shaman is given certain healing tools to work with — both in a physical sense and in the non-physical, invisible dimensions. For instance, I use a feather given to me by my Cherokee teacher many years ago. I also use a black jade sphere that I hold in my hand when I journey for information and pieces. I have another feather I use to "suck" out a block in a person's aura. I will also use my hands directly on a person's body if the block is so thick and large that it cannot be cut out, dug out, removed with the use of my large feather or sucked out via my other feather. Whatever block is removed, it is placed in a bowl of water. There are two bowls of water present during an extraction. One bowl is to take the block or "goo" removed from the individual. The second bowl is for the shaman to wash her/his hands, if necessary, during the "psychic surgery".

To give you an idea of how I work, I will journey first to ask my chief guide if s/he needs extraction. If my guide says "yes", they show me what has to be done and how to do it. Basically, after I get up on my knees and work over the client who is lying down and I am listening to my guide's instructions as to what to do.

I will run my hands about six inches above the client, moving from the top of the client's head to the bottom of their feet, feeling for hot or cold spots, which may indicate blocks or problem areas. I then use the narrow edge of the feather to make surgical incisions into the person's aura. Once the auric field(s) are open, I may use the tip of the feather to reach in, dip into the off-color "goo" (which can be thin, watery, thick or almost glue-like in consistency) and shake it off into the designated bowl of water. I do this again and again until the region is "clean". I then use another side of the feather to close the auric field(s) much like sutures.

If there is a small block, I will cut it open with the feather, place the other feather tip into the goo and then suck on the quill end with my lips. Once the goo is sucked up onto the feather, I shake it over the bowl of water to get rid of the substance. I will then go back and suck some more, if it is required. I then close up the aura with the larger feather.

The last way I work is by cutting open the aura with the feather and then using my hands to pull out the massive amounts of goo that have collected in a certain part of the person's aura. Whenever we are out of balance or harmony with ourselves, in whatever auric field it involves, positive ions begin to gather, much like water collecting in a balloon. In this case, the auric field is the balloon, and the positive ions are the water. The auric field begins to swell or collect positive ions. Over time, they can congeal into a dark looking block of energy that prevents healthy prana or negative ions from getting into our chakras and circulated through the auric fields. This creates illness. So, I see this collection of positive ions as "goo", something that should be removed in order to help a person maintain a higher level of health.

I will use both hands to scoop up huge quantities of the goo, and then release the substance I have collected into the bowl of water. I may have to do this one to four times before all the substance is removed from an area. I then wash my hands in the second bowl of clean water and close up the area with my feather.

After the extractions are completed, I shake my gourd rattle, clockwise, around the client four times to seal up their aura. The rattle encloses and protects the client as well as the work done that is done. The client's eyes are closed during this procedure and they are laying face up. They may feel the pulling, tugging or releasing of the block or thought form from their body or, they may feel nothing.

There may also be some other physical sensations connected with the psychic operation. When I performed extraction on Cindy to repair the damage to her navel and root chakra (the very places from where her alcoholic father had stolen her energy from), I removed a lot of very thick, tar-like goo from her abdominal region. I also had to cut

21

open, with the use of a feather, the auric field above her physical breasts. By removing the positive ions (goo) from the astral field (the one that contains our emotions), I was removing the block that helped to create the cysts in her breasts. With the removal of the block, the cysts, in most cases, will disappear in time. Fat globules could be seen in each breast — those were the cysts that she'd had all her life. Afterward, Cindy experienced cramp-like pains in the abdominal area, plus nausea. The extraction was performed at 10 p.m. that night, and the cramping lasted until 2 a.m. the next morning.

It is not unusual, especially when working with the solar plexus or navel chakra, for the client to experience nausea or vomiting shortly after the extraction. This is a good sign that the healing "took". The physical sensations rarely last more than twenty-four hours.

Wherever extraction is performed that region will begin to heal itself, and the client will find an amazing return to health afterward.

CHAPTER 2

SOUL RECOVERY:

THE BEGINNING

When I finished taking Oh Shinnah Fast Wolf's crystal and gem healing studies in 1986, I went home to Ohio to eagerly utilize these new healing techniques on my clients who were interested in experiencing a wholistic approach. Originally, I had been helping them with homeopathy, diet, vitamins and mineral suggestions. An interesting phenomena began evolving as I worked in a client's aura. The work was supposed to be at arm's length; I didn't have to place my hands on them in a physical sense.

Although the crystal was to be used within the client's aura, my spirit guides (who have the guise/shape of animals) kept instructing me to place my hands on the client's shoulders. I resisted this suggestion a number of times, until I had a powerful event occur one day during meditation.

I usually meditated every day for at least thirty to forty-five minutes. One of my main spirit guides, a female silver-tipped grizzly bear, popped in whenever I meditated. Usually, she just sat in the room. This time, she ambled over to where I lay on the floor and told me not to be afraid. I did not have time to ask, "afraid of what?"

The bear moved to my head and slipped her body over mine, much like a hand is covered with a glove. The sensation was very different, even uncomfortable because I had never experienced such a thing before The bear told me to relax and adjust to this new sensation. After five minutes, she gently slipped off me, much like taking a glove off a hand — only she was the glove and I was the hand.

After coming out of meditation, I asked the bear what

she had done. She told me that I had "become" her. In other words, I took on the shape of her. She said this was another way to heal, and that if I wanted to try it this way, I could. Of course, as always, she left the choice up to me; she would never initiate such a change unless I approved. It was another way to assist me in helping to move the energy to heal the client. "A more direct way," she said with certainty.

She informed me that in order to do this method, at first, that I would have to lay my hands on the client's shoulders and close my eyes as I stood behind them. She then asked if I would like to try this on my next client and see the results of our mutual bonding. My curiosity was piqued. The bear had been my teacher, guide and protector for four years, and I had no reason to distrust this new method she was teaching me. It was obvious to me she felt it was time to move into this new realm of healing, so I agreed to her suggestion.

I could hardly wait until next Wednesday when I performed the healings for those who came. Understand that one person never heals another person. It is simply that the healer opens herself up to the higher energies and forces (the Cherokee refer to these as the Grandparents, the Great Mystery or Spirit), and steps aside so these can be transferred to the client. I was nothing more than a conduit through which the energy flowed. The next week came and I was ready. My spirit guide came over me after I laid hands on the shoulders of one of my female clients. As I looked at my arm, it was covered with thick, silver-tipped black fur.

Once I adjusted to the situation, my bear told me to look through her eyes. As I focused my inner vision through her eyes, there was the sensation of looking through a microscope or Coke bottles. It took me a few moments to adjust my eyes.

After settling in with the different sensations, the bear invited me to look into the person. I realized, with another start, that I was no longer seeing third dimensionally, but fourth dimensionally. The bear told me to follow her eye movements — we began to look inside the client. I was amazed.

I saw the client's entire inner organ and bone structure. I saw each organ as it was working, the arteries, veins, tendons, muscles and bones. It was as if I was seeing every-thing better than any state-of-the-art CAT scan. Plus, it was in living color! I noted that the woman's liver had a greenish-yellow cloud around it, and my bear mentally con-firmed my observation.

The bear told me that the woman's liver was ailing, and that this was a "red flag" of danger to me about the organ's state of dysfunction. It told me the client was ill in this area of her body. I became very excited and started sweeping our vision throughout the client's body. To my surprise, in the intestines in the left quadrant of the abdomen, I saw a red, gnome-like man hiding among them.

I asked my bear if I was seeing right, or was I imagining the whole thing. She told me that humans hold blocks within their physical body and their aura; however, they may be symbolic thought forms. These blocks or thought form symbols were suppressed or repressed emotions trauma or shock that the organ(s), connective tissue, muscle or bone remembered and still was held within it or them.

Fascinated, I asked my bear how one could get rid of such pests. I felt her smile. The gnome was standing up in the woman's intestines, cursing at me and shaking his fist, his face red as a beet. He was angry and threatening me, wanting me to leave him alone. I again asked bear how to remove such a symbolic block.

She told me that my spirit guide hawk could remove the gnome. All I had to do was instruct the hawk to move the gnome to a dimension where he could never hurt this woman again and to take it to a place that was for its highest spiritual good.

I asked my hawk to do exactly that, and through bear's eyes, I saw her swoop down, talons extended and grab the angry little gnome. She flew up and out of the woman and then blipped into invisibility, into another dimension. She returned moments later without the nasty little gnome.

When we were done with the woman, and my bear had disengaged herself from around me, I talked to the woman. She told me that she had been having a lot of trouble with diarrhea and had been diagnosed with IBS (irritable bowel syndrome). I was delighted with the confirmation and did not tell her what I saw or did. The happy ending to this story was that the woman stopped having IBS symptoms, and her bowel movements returned to normal. Further, the liver was healed and she no longer had digestion problems she previously blamed on her stomach.

I did not tell my client what was done to her because I wasn't sure she would believe me! I was having trouble believing it myself at that time. However, the woman's IBS went away within several weeks of the healing, so I knew something was happening that was positive, regardless of whether the client or myself could really grasp how the healing had happened.

My bear taught me a great deal more in the ensuing months as I worked with my Wednesday clients. My other spirit guides began to bring "pieces" back to these people, as well as take things out of their body or out of their aura.

As I continued crystal healings over the next year, I would automatically, at the end of the crystal portion, place my hands on the client's shoulders and the bear would come over me. The bear never discussed what it was that I was being taught and what I was a conduit for, and I never asked. I trusted my spirit guides with my life, and with the lives of others, implicitly. I did not need to give this method a label. It worked, and that was the bottom line.

In 1990, after I had moved to Arizona, I met a woman therapist whom I'll call Sally. She was from Europe, and had been trained shamanically by her spirit guides over a course of twenty years. Sally had learned these techniques and employed them regularly with her clients during therapy sessions. Interested, I shared with her what I had been taught by my bear years before. She confirmed that what I had been taught was very similar to what she had been taught. Both of us had led shamanic lives, in that we'd nearly died several times, and both of us had come from highly metaphysical families where psychic gifts were passed on generation to generation. She had Gypsy blood, and I had some Native American blood.

Needless to say, I was delighted with this "double check" and realized that the Grandparents had placed Sally on my path to educate me about what I was doing.

I gave a great deal of thought to the fact I was helping to bring back soul pieces to a person via my industrious and very busy spirit guides. The extraction was equally important. After comparing methods with Sally, I realized that I had been trained a little differently than she had. I had been taught ways that she had not, and vice versa. I will not go into the differences because the methods are well-guarded secrets known only to those who are supposed to be practicing these talents and skills. The fact that I had received my training from the "other side" was, for me personally, a far greater validation than having learned it on "this side" through a physical teacher.

However, I do not devalue a person learning these methods from a human teacher. In the Indian sense, "the old way," the way that was most powerful and respected, was to be taught by one's spirit guide(s). When it is done in this fashion, it means that the person is ready to develop and move into this area.

People drawn to perform soul recovery and extraction may not be ready for such a heavy responsibility, despite their good intentions. A spirit guide will never teach someone shamanistic ways unless they are ready to learn. Unfortunately, a spirit guide cannot make someone work positively, humbly or with humanitarian leanings.

Over the years, I've had many people write and ask me to teach them the method I was taught, and have passed on to my facilitators. I will not do this. If a person is truly to learn about shamanism, my opinion is that it will happen through a series of events over a long period of time, plus they must have the 'death' experience or the 'wounded healer' experience to qualify them, too. If you are in a hurry, or can't accept this advice, then go to Michael Harner and learn his methods. The name of his foundation, address and phone number is in the additional information section at the end of the book.

Some people will learn shamanism in order to learn about the use or abuse of power, and may not be temperamentally suited to be a shaman. Egos have no place in the healing arts — only humility and humbleness — because, when you realize that you really are not doing anything except being a transit or tube through which the energy flows to the client, you cannot take much credit, can you?

WHAT IS SHAMANISM?

Ten thousand years ago, men and women from cultures from around the world who had the special ability to "fly" or leave their body to move into the unseen worlds around them to journey for their client/patient were known as shamans. Today, shamanism is practiced around the world by many diverse cultures, including Native Americans in both North, Central and South America.

In modern-day terms, shamanism involves the ability to switch from the left hemisphere of our brain, which keeps us completely grounded in this third dimension where we live, to the right hemisphere. Here we can achieve an altered state in order to pierce through all the other dimensions that surround us at all times.

The word "fly" is a misnomer, because the shaman does not leave the body as an outer experience per astral projection or an out-of-body experience. Instead, the shaman switches to the right brain which is "hooked up" to all the other dimensions simultaneously and begins an inner journey by "flying" to these other worlds/dimensions/places to find lost parts of an individual's soul.

The shaman has the ability to disconnect, at will, from the grounding roots of the left brain/third dimensional world and move into the right brain. It is important to remember that a shaman controls this skill and does it at will.

One who has no control over this switching process between brain hemispheres is known as being a schizophrenic. These people see, hear, smell, taste and feel all the dimensions simultaneously. Of course, the schizophrenic has massive soul loss. However, they can return to the third dimension once the shaman finds those pieces and brings them back.

There is a difference between a medicine person and a shaman. A medicine person cannot "fly" or capture pieces of a person's soul that were taken or "stuck" in a certain time frame of the person's existence. Conversely, a shaman may or may not be a medicine person. Usually, the two metaphysical "trades" are unique unto themselves, and few are skilled in both arenas and disciplines. Some shaman-based cultures incorporate the use of hallucinogenic drugs to achieve the necessary altered state. For instance, the Huichol Indians of Baja, Mexico use peyote to enter the altered state to reach the other dimensional worlds.

FINDING THE RIGHT SHAMAN

Name references aside, I agreed wholeheartedly with Sally that our methods should not be taught indiscriminately to just anyone because great harm, even death, can be inflicted by that individual once they know the method. On the down side, a shaman can use their power negatively; they then become known as a sorcerer.

They become what I call "power stalkers", shadowing people who have true power, which they want to steal because they want more than their own personal power. If they are taught SR/E, they become a loose cannon on the deck, able to inflict great injury by stealing parts of an unknowing person's soul, causing great damage to the person's aura or sending symbolic thought forms into the person's physical body to wreak havoc or injury.

This down side to SR/E needs discussion because people drawn to have this method of healing performed on them need guidelines. They must know how to discern a power stalker and sorcerer from a healer who morally knows and respects your boundaries when using such a technique.

A client who wants SR/E performed should ask the following questions:

1. Where did you learn SR/E? Right now, Michael Harner's foundation is the only organization teaching this method. If the shaman you are considering to do your SR/E is a Harner graduate, call 203/454-2825 (the Harner Foundation) and ask for references on this shaman. Also ask the shaman for references of people s/he has performed SR/E on.

Then, call each reference and ask if the person was satisfied with whoever performed SR/E on them. Ask if they have gotten better due to the SR/E. If they are worse, or if they are experiencing extreme fatigue, exhaustion or tiredness ever since the journey, avoid this individual. It is not uncommon shortly after a journey or extraction to feel tiredness or fatigue for up to a week afterward. This is because the aura and physical body is readjusting to the returned pieces and/or extraction. However, if this state of continual tiredness or loss of energy continues for months after seeing a shaman, then something is drastically wrong.

Knowing SR/E can enable the sorcerer to literally place umbilical cords (or lines) into another's aura and begin draining them of energy — on a continuous, twenty-four hour a day basis. Further, when SR/E is done correctly, the person will, within three months be in much better health on all levels. Sometimes, it is only a matter of twelve hours after the SR/E is performed, and the client feels one hundred percent better. Sometimes, it is 48 to 72 hours. Sometimes, it takes the entire three months for the soul pieces to integrate back into the person's consciousness. Each person is different as to the time frame. The bottom is this: if you are worse than before this person performed the SR/E, you should not allow that individual to perform it on you again!

2. Your second line of defense is YOU. When you talk to the person who does SR/E, what is your instinctive response to this person? Do you feel good about them? Do you like their energy? Do you like what they have to say

about SR/E? Your best defense is your own inner know-
ing/voice. Unfortunately, many people distrust their own
inner guidance system.

3. If the person is not Harner trained, again, request
references from them. Call these client references and ask
the same questions as suggested in #1. If you get a mixed
response, or your gut warns you to stay away from this
individual that performs SR/E, then stay way!

4. Ask how the person performing SR/E was trained if
they were not a Harner graduate. The best answer is that
they were trained by their own guides. If it is an outside
teacher, ask for the name of the teacher and a phone number. Talk to this teacher and get a "vibe" on them. If it feels
good, and all the questions are answered positively and to
your satisfaction, then you may want SR/E performed.

Your best source of information on someone who performs SR/E is people who have had it done to them by this
individual. Unfortunately, there are no stringent laws or
guidelines in place for those who perform SR/E. Karmically,
anyone who practices SR/E for the highest good of the client
is in the hands of not only their guides, but the client's chief
guide, too.

Be aware that a shaman who performs SR/E never makes
judgments during this process — but always does what their
guides or the client's guides direct the shaman to do or
accomplish. This way, the shaman does not incur needless
karma from this client or vice versa.

Sorcerers do not care about karma and will do anything
they feel like doing to the client — stealing energy or stealing soul pieces from them. Eventually, in some lifetime, the
sorcerer will receive the karma they deserve.

Another function of a shaman who practices SR/E is to
deal with sorcerers who have "plugged" into a client. A
shaman can take back soul pieces that belong to the client.

On a reservation someone, usually a power stalker or
sorcerer, will be paid to smoke a pipe against an unsuspect-
ing person. The person's health begins to deteriorate unless
they get to a medicine person or shaman to rectify the

situation.

When asked to intervene on these cases, I have had to seek out the person who smoked the pipe against my client, break the pipe (in a spiritual sense) and render it useless and take back any piece(s) that the pipe smoker may have stolen from this person. At other times, when a pipe was not involved, but a sorcerer was, I had to deal with them and get back the stolen pieces.

Let me say that this type of soul thievery is perhaps five percent of all SR/E that I have performed on individuals. It is not a rampant thing; nor should you worry about this. Just be sure you choose a shaman who has very high morals, values and principles with respect to utilizing this method on your behalf.

If you get a bad vibe, if you are uncomfortable or you are not sure about this individual, **do not do it!** In the back of this book is a glossary of students who have learned SR/E from me, along with their addresses so that you can contact them if you wish. The Foundation of Shamanic Studies is also included in case you feel the Harner method is the best path of healing for you.

All methods work and all are a little different because of each tribe or tribal nation's beliefs being a bit different. However, SR/E usually relies on certain tools in order to initiate the healing.

All SR/E methods involve spirit guides (called power animals by Harner) who are usually in the guise of an animal, insect, reptile, etc. To achieve the altered state, shamans from around the world utilize different tools to reach that state.

Harner's method, as mine, does not incorporate the use of drugs. Instead, we both rely on an outside/external source to create the energy necessary to make the conscious shift from left brain to right brain. That tool is the drum.

THE DRUM

The drum is the shaman's tool to open up the dimensions in the right brain that will make a journey possible.

Usually, the type of drum used to achieve the altered state is the hand-held variety. The drums are hand made from trees for the wooden frame and the use of the skin of an animal (goat, deer, cow or elk) as a hide to cover the surface and frame of the drum.

They can be made by Native Americans or anyone who is drawn to make them. The drum is a living being, from the wood that is used to make the frame, to the hide of the animal who has given its life to make the drum. From the Cherokee standpoint, we treat our drums as living, viable beings that have a clear intelligence, personality and certain skills, talents or powers — just like any human being. We have a name for each drum, which we keep secret, and we know the drum's capacity and capabilities.

The actual drumming (a moderate beat) creates the tonal frequency that parallel's Mother Earth's heartbeat. Since we are her children (as is everything on her), we respond to that frequency on an unconscious level, just as does any baby when she is pressed against her mother's heart.

Once we relax and allow the frequency of the beat to move us consciously from the left to right brain, the leap to the altered state is accomplished.

During an SR/E, there is usually a shaman and an assistant who is the drummer. Sometimes the shaman carries a cassette drumming tape, puts on the headphones and travels without the help of an assistant.

The shaman who is able to perform SR/E can have different levels of skills. For instance, when I first was taught this via my bear, I did all SR/E in person with the client. Now, years later, I can have my mother, Ruth, drum for me, move into the altered state and perform SR/E on a client who lives half way around the world.

Long distance journeying is a special skill, and not all shamans have that ability. However, all my associates are fully capable of laying down, taking a journey half way around the world to help an individual. Extraction is done with equal success. It is not any less effective than if it were done in person, plus it saves the client tremendous time and money. One does not need to fly or travel to see the shaman — we can journey to you through the other dimensions to affect healing. The same steps for healing are followed, only we visualized them in the other worlds for you.

I used to do all extractions in person with the client next to me. Now, I can do extractions "long distance" — anywhere in the world. As the shaman develops their skills, it will be possible for them to do the SR/E long distance. Before an SR/E, whether it is in person or long distance, I smudge not only myself, but the drum and assistant with sacred sage, which is gathered ceremonially. I also smudge the client, if present. This smudging cleanses our auras of positive ions, which are like accumulated dust, and cleans us up — much like a surgeon washing their hands before surgery.

THE THREE WORLDS OF THE SHAMAN

When I was being taught SR/E, I noticed that sometimes I was taken to a dark place; in another world, it was bright, white light; and yet in a third world, it resembled our everyday existence here in the third dimension. I had no names for these places. There were even times when I was taken into a client's past life to retrieve a missing piece, and I did not realize it until after I came out of the altered state and analyzed what had happened or discussed it with the client.

The **DARK WORLD** is always reached via a tree trunk, or any hole in the ground, and I go down through the root system deep into Mother Earth herself. This is the place I was shown to retrieve spirit guides for people, plus a place where dead human spirits chose to stay. It is a dark, swampy area with a beautiful series of gem-encrusted caves and lovely, colorful scenery ranging from mountains to oceans and jungles. I call it the Dark World only because I had to enter it by going down through a dark tunnel.

The Dark World is Mother Earth's realm and on three separate occasions I have been invited to her cave to see her for a client. It is an overwhelming emotional experience to talk with her directly, to feel her endless/boundless love that she has for all her children. On those journeys for my clients, she had gifts that she wanted me to give to them. For me, it is an honor to even be allowed to visit her!

Often, a soul who has died but not given back the pieces of others that they still have in their possession, will choose to remain in the Dark World. At times, when I have come to ask for that piece back from this lost soul, I will ask if s/he wants to give back all remaining pieces in his possession to the individual they have taken them from. Sometimes they will say yes, and sometimes they refuse my offer. If they do want to "unload" these pieces, I return them to each individual, and then help the soul up into the Light World.

I love to go to the Dark World because it puts me in close contact with Mother Earth, my real mother. I always feel vibrantly and warmly loved whenever I go there on a journey. Sometimes (not often), I will journey and play with my spirit guides on a slope of a mountain meadow that is surrounded by dark evergreens and colorful wildflowers dotting the area. The Dark World is a restful place for me, and gives me the opportunity to relax, talk at length with my spirit guides (who also prefer this realm) and in general, play.

Each shaman has a place to go to "recharge". I cannot speak for other shamans and where or if they go anywhere for a rest or recharging. I do know that the Dark World is my healing place whenever I get out of balance with my own energies, or if I need a break. Looking at it logically, I am a woman, and Mother Earth is not only my mother, she is female.

The **LIGHT WORLD** is analogous with Christianity's heaven. When I first was taken there to get a piece of some one's soul, I was nearly blinded by the white radiance of the light — only because I had been totally unprepared for it. The light is bright, but not blinding. To zoom out of the Dark World, riding on my hawk's back and in a split second be in the Light World takes a bit of adjustment.

The Light World is where all souls who have died go on to learn new skills, rest or wait for other loved ones to cross the Rainbow Bridge (death). No one's soul can move into the Light unless they have given back all the pieces they have taken from others.

Sometimes I go to the Light World to talk to a client's chief guide. It should be mentioned that everyone has any number of guides. I always single out the head honcho or what I refer to as the chief guide. However, a chief guide can be found in any of the three worlds. Before I journey, my chief guide will appear to me and give me instructions for the client, which I follow to the letter. Everyone has a chief guide and a panel of other teachers or guides. It does not matter whether you are a shaman or not — they are there. A shaman never willingly talks about their guides, what they are, their names or anything connected to or about them. To do so is considered bragging and egotistical. For the sake of this book, I have discussed some of mine within the context of the material presented, but otherwise, would never think of discussing them.

The chief guide may give me a message to give to the client, or may give me a "gift" to bring back to them. For instance, on one journey, a set of transparent blue beads were given to me to give to this man with instructions to place them (invisible to the third dimension's physical set of eyes) around his neck. His guide, a lovely young woman dressed in a long, blue gown, told me to tell him that this would not only protect his throat chakra, but would help him to speak out and communicate better — and this client was very closed up and uncommunicative. Since receiving this gift, he's been writing me letters and communicating at such a rate I can hardly keep up with him!

Another area of the Light World I recently was introduced to was a beautiful, radiant lake. I was retrieving pieces for a female client when I was taken to this lake. According to my hawk guide, in this lake there were "pieces of light" that were miscarried or aborted babies. I dove into the lake and was shown which soul piece belonged to this client and brought it back to her.

It is not unusual for a piece of a person's soul to fly off while in their mother's womb due to the mother being traumatized in an auto accident, a fall, an emotional trauma of any sort or a physical illness. A piece may fly off during the birthing procedure (because the labor was long, drug induced or traumatic), or the piece could fly off shortly after birth because the soul knows it has a very rough life ahead with a lot of pain and it wants to escape that pain. The soul piece escapes by flying back to the Light World — a place of safety and protection.

The female client I retrieved this "piece of light" for in the lake in the Light World told me that she had a miscarriage and that she had grieved deeply over the loss of her baby. She had miscarried four weeks after conception, so the piece I returned looked like a blob of white, shining Jello.

I was very interested in this Lake of Lost Children (as I call it). Hawk told me later that the souls of those miscarried or aborted babies come here — how beautiful — to a lake of warm, clean, clear water that resembles the water of a mother's womb.

There is a wonderful book on soul pieces called *Soul Retrieval* by Sandra Ingerman (HarperCollins). We keep copies of it on hand in case anyone wants to order it directly from us.

I highly recommend Ingerman's book as a companion to this one. Each gives unique and different information about the soul realm and how we lose our pieces. Sandra Ingerman had taken Harner's courses in core shamanism. Today, she is the director of education at the foundation and has done the world a great service by writing compassionately, and in clearly understood terms, about soul fragmentation and loss.

Ingerman writes about the Cave of the Lost Children in the Dark World, where abused, battered, sexually molested or abandoned children's soul pieces go for safety. I have never gone there, never seen it, but I do believe that such a place in the Dark World can certainly exist. It is interesting to me that a parallel to it is found in the Light World. As above, so below.

I am often taken up to the Light World to speak to a client's deceased relative or friend — either from this lifetime or another lifetime. Usually, I bring back messages for the client, and on occasion, a gift that will help the client get through this particular harrowing part of their life. Most often, it is a message that is brought to the client that has great personal meaning to them.

Some shamans have a hard time returning from the Light World because the intense love that surrounds them makes it doubly tough to come back to our third dimensional world where such feeling and energy does not exist. I know one shaman who will spend hours a day languishing in the Light World, neglecting her duties in the third dimensional world because she prefers the energy there.

However, this does not solve the problems she is supposed to be working through. Personally, I never go there unless it is for a soul piece, to talk to the person's guide, a deceased loved one or to take a gift back to the client.

The **REAL WORLD** looks like and is our third dimensional existence. Most frequently, I find souls who have died, but who are keeping pieces of others here in this world. I also find people who are alive in this world who have pieces of the client.

The Real World is where most of us have lost pieces due to trauma or emotional shock of some kind. It is the place where most soul theft takes place, because the person who takes a piece of you is living as well.

However, if a person from a past life has a piece of you, the shaman can travel via the Real World into that past life and find that piece and retrieve it for you. I will also add, but not go into detail, that a shaman can also move "forward" into future lifetimes of a client if necessary.

Let me give an example of how the Real World operates. If a child of six is in an auto accident, a piece of her flies off and lodges in that time of her life. She recuperates from the accident and continues on, but that piece of her remains "stuck" in that time warp of trauma. A shaman can go back in time and bring the piece home to the client.

There are other worlds I have traversed that do not have any name or label on them, either. At times, I have journeyed through galaxies, visited other planets, other beings far outside of our known galaxy and universe. I am sure there are other worlds beyond what I have thus far experienced.

Shamans are not dealing with linear time when in an altered state. Time is not from point A to point B. It is like a stack of pancakes, piled up on top of one another. We can go journey through many different worlds — thanks to the help and guidance of our spirit guides — and bring back soul pieces for our client. Most importantly, the shaman does this at will and without drugs.

SR/E is truly one of the most powerful healing tools.

CHAPTER 3

CASE HISTORIES OF SOUL RECOVERY AND EXTRACTION

The cases that are presented below are true. The clients have asked that their names be changed to protect their privacy, and we have complied.

CASE # 1, by Ai Gvhdi Waya

Bonita is a lively, talkative woman of forty-five. She has two grown daughters who still live with her, and a husband of twenty plus years. Her voice is a very high, falsetto "little girl" voice despite her age and height (5'10"). She has had chronic bouts of depression on and off throughout her life. She remembers being sexually molested by her half-sister's husband. However, she has very little memory of life before ten years old. Bonita has had bouts of depression since age 30. On the last depression, she went from a size 16 to size 8 and has remained pencil thin.

When Bonita called me and asked me to perform SR/E long distance, she was, in my personal opinion, in the midst of a powerful change of individuation that happens to all of us in our mid-forties. The problem with Bonita was that she came from the old concept of believing all she could do was to be a housewife, cook for the family, clean and have no life of her own. It was all catching up with her and I had frequently seen depression as a consequence of this. I also knew her sexual molestation had given her the unconscious message: you are only a woman, you are not worthy and you do not count. Further, Bonita's self esteem was completely destroyed, as was her confidence and ability to trust her own sense of herself as an individual and as a woman.

Typical of a sexually molested woman, Bonita had many male friends and disdained friendships or closeness with women — this is the captor/captive psychology that often occurs after a molestation or rape. Because Bonita did not trust herself as a woman, she had no trust in other women. However, she had trust in men who had broken her trust. This is not an unusual scenario, and it told me where Bonita was "at" before I went on the SR/E journey for her.

Because of the low trust factor with women, I told Bonita that I would choose to do her SR and possibly, E, in the following two week period at night. I work best at night, regardless of whether it is long distance or with the client physically beside me (all facilitators are different and some work best during the day, or other time frames). Women are in their power at night, just as men are in their power during the daylight hours. I asked when Bonita went to bed — 10 p.m., and so noted it in her file.

About one and a half weeks later, I felt the time was right to journey for Bonita. My mother drummed for me as I laid down and closed my eyes. In my right hand was the black jade sphere I always "traveled" with because it provided an anchoring energy back into the third dimension should I ever get into trouble on a journey — and there can be plenty of danger to the shaman on some trips. However, I had my spirit guides with me and I flew to Bonita's house.

As I entered her bedroom, I saw her still in her clothes, laying on her right side, with her hands beneath her cheek and her legs pulled up toward her body — almost in a fetal position. I noted she lay on the left side of bed if one were facing it from the footboard. I mentally "clicked" this picture for later use as a double check with Bonita.

My chief guide came in, an Indian woman who will remain unnamed, and told me that I had permission to find Bonita's soul pieces. She sent me and my hawk flying into the Dark World.

We flew through darkness so thick I could not see may hand in front of my face. I saw blips of this ten months old baby in a crib, violently kicking her feet outward, as if to ward off or fight off someone. I could not see because the blackness literally surrounded all but that spotlight shining on her crib. I asked if she was Bonita, and she said yes. As I stood there, I sensed a dangerous male presence in the darkness and realized she sensed it too. She was trying to defend herself the only way she could under the circumstances. I asked if she wanted to come home to Bonita — that she had grown and really needed her back now. The baby instantly lifted her arms toward me and I scooped her out of the crib, mounted my hawk and we were off! I deposited the ten-month old beside the sleeping Bonita and waited to see where my chief guide would send me next.

I next journeyed into the Real World, and I saw Bonita's husband in slacks, a white, long-sleeved shirt and tie. He was sitting at his desk working. As I popped into his office, he looked up at me with a strange expression on his face. He knew why I had come. I asked him if he had a piece of Bonita. Sheepishly, he nodded his head and his face took on the look of a beaten dog. With a grimace, he pulled out a heart locket on a gold chain and handed it to me — this was the piece of Bonita he had taken. As he gave it to me, he muttered, almost embarrassed to admit it, "I'm afraid I'll lose her love by giving this back to her."

"No, you'll have a better chance of having her stay now that you gave back what didn't belong to you," I told him gently. I slipped a rose quartz heart into his hand, telling him that this would take the place of the soul piece he was returning. He looked lost and almost frightened when I left with the heart-shaped locket necklace in hand.

I placed the locket beside sleeping Bonita and waited to see if we had to go elsewhere. We again journeyed into the Real World. This time, I popped in on a scene where I saw Bonita around the age of 6 to 8 years old. She was wearing a long ponytail and a cute, flowery print cotton dress. With her were two of her friends. The look on Bonita's face was one of pure terror. I looked in that direction and saw this tall, rawboned kind of man, with rugged features and an

Elvis Presley haircut — only he had light brown hair — standing there watching Bonita intently, like a wolf waiting to jump his chosen prey. We were on a playground, and I could feel this man stalking Bonita. I realized that this was the man who was sexually molesting her.

I asked Bonita if she wanted to leave with me and come back to the grown-up version of herself. Instantly, she said yes. Before I took the piece back to Bonita, I turned to the man who was looking at me with outrage, and asked if he would leave Bonita alone. He adamantly refused. He said it was his right to take a piece of Bonita any time he felt like it. I had no business trying to tell him what to do.

From long experience with belligerent individuals like this who won't give their word to leave their victim alone, I "trap" them in a web of their own making. A spider web entrapped the man. He tried to escape, shouting and yelling obscenities at me. He even threatened to kill me if I didn't release him.

Grimly, I walked within a few feet of him and told him that once he decided to never molest anyone again in this lifetime, the spider web would instantly melt away and he would be free. However, if he refused to give his word, he would remain trapped there for as long as it took him to realize it was not his privilege or right to sexually harm any person — child or adult.

I picked up Bonita's soul piece and we flew back to where Bonita was sleeping. I turned to my chief guide and before I could ask if there were anymore pieces to retrieve, my hawk and I were caught up in this blackness. I figured it was the Dark World — I figured wrong.

We popped into an English home that was lit with a taper. I saw an older man with long, white sideburns, a set of small, Benjamin Franklin glasses perched on the end of his bulbous nose. On the desk in front of him was a feather quill in an ink pot with several books to the left of him. He was reading something, and I saw that he was sitting in a library with a lot of leather bound books. It was very dark and dim except around the desk. I noticed he wore a black waistcoat and pants, and that his white shirt had a cleric's collar on it. I asked if he had a piece of Bonita, and he lifted his massive head and stared at me in silence. He reached into the left breast pocket of his waistcoat and drew out a cloth dolly. I thanked him. He looked awfully sad.

I knew he was dead, whoever he was, and asked if there was anything I could do for him. I figured he was "stuck" in the Real World time frame because he had other pieces of other people yet, so could not move to the Light World. Sometimes, if I feel right about it, I will ask the spirit if they would like me to return the pieces to whom they belong and help them get into the Light.

This man sadly shook his head and said nothing. I thanked him, gave him the rose quartz heart and left. When I arrived back at Bonita's bedroom, I blew each piece I had brought back into her heart chakra and crown chakra. I then performed extraction on her at the request of her chief guide.

From her heart chakra, I pulled out a lot of black, tar-like goo. The heart region was so congested that I had serious concerns that she was a candidate for a heart attack.

I cut open her abdomen and extracted a huge amount of viscous black gel. I noted her small intestines had a dull orange color to them, which is not the healthy color they should be.

My spirit guide pointed to Bonita's neck, and I stared in shock. There, around her throat was a shackle! I did not know how I was going to get it off her until Bonita's guide handed me the key to unlock it. I removed the shackle and then worked on her brow chakra where I removed some dark black material.

As I stood back, my guide pointed to Bonita's shoulders. There was what appeared to be a thick, dark gray blanket hovering over each shoulder about one foot thick. I removed this material. I then enclosed her with gold light to protect her and then came back to my own body.

After coming out of the altered state, I quickly wrote down the information I received and typed up the report as soon as possible. The next morning I called Bonita with the results.

When I told her about the ten-month-old baby, she said that made a lot of sense because her molester was around her from the time she had been born into the family, and he hung around a lot. Bonita said he could have come into her room, watched her, thought about molesting her, or perhaps did molest her at that young age. Bonita has no recall of this occurring, and I assured her that now the piece was back, the memory would slowly surface.

As I told her I had obtained a heart locket on a necklace from her husband, she gasped. Her husband's gifts to her over the years were always necklaces — which Bonita refuses to wear. She hates to wear anything around her neck. I feel on a subconscious level that she saw the necklace as a symbol of a dog's collar. She felt chained enough to her husband and the stifling and imprisoning situation without wearing his necklace gifts, too.

When I described her sexual molester, Bonita had no memory of what her molester looked like. It is normal for someone to blank out what the attacker looks like. I told her that she would start to remember him now that this piece had returned.

She gasped again as I told her about the old man in a black frock with a cleric collar. According to her husband, who is a genealogy expert, Bonita's side of the family came from England and several of her forbears had been Protestant ministers. It was then that I realized that I had tripped back into one of Bonita's past lifetimes, and gone to the man who still had a piece of her. We were both astounded by this discovery.

Whenever I journey for someone, I do not want to know why they want me to journey ahead of time. I like to journey "cold", without any information to mess up my head. By going in without knowing anything, the double check to my client and myself is very powerful and confirming. I had no idea that Bonita's side of the family had clergymen from England.

On the extraction, the oddest thing happened twenty-four hours afterward. Bonita called me up the next morning and said that her high, falsetto voice was gone. In its place was slightly deep, husky voice — one that she had always wanted — but now that the shackle that had been placed around her throat/larynx was gone, her voice dropped several octaves! I heard the tonal difference in her voice, and it has remained that way since the extraction.

Bonita had ten to fifteen minutes of nausea and complained of an upset stomach the afternoon after the extraction. I told her this was a good sign that the surgery in the abdominal area "took". She has had no recurrence of the nausea since that one episode.

I asked Bonita if she had bowel problems or diarrhea because I had seen the unhealthy color of her small intestines. She said no, she had experienced no problems. My assessment was that if the cleaning of her bowel region had not taken place, she would have had those problems at a later date.

I asked about her heart region — did it feel different. She said it felt "lighter" and that she had experienced some moments of heart palpitations. This is normal when a chakra is cleared and starting to spin once again. There is a natural adjustment that occurs in the physical body, too, but it will never create any damage or injury. It was a double check to me that the heart chakra, once cleaned, was now operating smoothly and the heart palpitations signaled a return to health. Bonita never had any more palpitations beyond the first twenty-four hour period after the extraction.

With every journey and every extraction, I learn something new. This was the second time I had been thrown into a past life without realizing it. I am going to have to clear up this confusion with my guides and have them alert me to the fact that I am crossing from present into past, or present into future.

I also learned that Mary Buckner performed soul repair on one of her clients, and the client (a long distance one) called her up in amazement the next morning to report that her voice had deepened!! This is the second case where I have seen a voice change, but I am not surprised. The woman did not have a shackle on her throat, as Bonita did. But whatever piece was missing and now returned, physically affected her voice.

CASE # 2, by Ardella Hecht

Animals have need for soul recovery and extraction just like people do. And, in the more than 1000 journeys I have done for various people around the world, I have also been asked by some of my clients to journey for their animals. People who realize their own need for soul recovery and extraction also realize the same need for the animals they love and care for.

I received a call from Sam who asked if I would journey for his cat, Samantha. He did not know what could have happened, she had always been very loving and went outside once in a while to roll in the grass. Sam explained that Samantha had always been a somewhat fearful cat, but lately would not even go outside. And, more recently Samantha took to urinating and spraying in the house. Sam did explain that he was preparing to move and Samantha had always been sensitive to any changes in her home environment, but never resorted to this. He asked if I could help her; and I said I would journey and see what our (mine and Samantha's) spirit guides would reveal to me. We set a date for me to journey and a time for him to call for the report.

When I journeyed, I received permission from our spirit guides and they led me to the following information: I was shown that Samantha had two soul pieces split off out of fear when she was a young kitten. The first soul piece left when she was taken from her mother. Her fear of abandonment and insecurity was more than what this sweet little thing could handle. Her soul piece gladly returned when I was taken to it. The second piece left when another animal entered Samantha's domain and frightened her. How like children to be threatened by the block bully. Her need at that time to spray and establish her domain programmed her to spray when she feels in a similar state of fear. This piece also gladly returned to Samantha. I was told this was all that was necessary to do at this time. I blew the pieces into her heart chakra and her crown chakra, and sealed her in golden light.

When Sam called me a couple of weeks later to report her progress, he said that she has not sprayed in the house since I journeyed for her. He was also very happy to report that she seemed less fearful, and was going outside for the first time in quite a while. I have talked to Sam a number of times since then on other matters, and he reports that Samantha is still doing great. She even made the move with no traumatic results and no further spraying. He was so glad to have his kitty back to her loving and playful self.

CASE # 3, by Karen David

Anna, a beautiful, tall woman in her late forties, came to me for soul retrieval. Reticent and soft spoken, Anna hesitantly told me of her need. She explained that she had been in counseling for the past six years and one of the main issues had been sexual abuse from her father. What she also wanted was to get a better understanding and handle on her intense need for control and feeling as if she had to always be perfect. Anna had mentioned that her life, although productive, did not feel as if it was a thriving existence. Even though she was fully aware of the abuse from childhood, she definitely felt there were still things missing. Anna did not "feel" the effects of therapy as much as she understood it intellectually. Consequently, she still felt numb.

While listening to her intently, I was aware of how much inner wisdom and love this woman possessed. Yet when I stared into her eyes, in their place was a look of emptiness. I also received the impression that she somehow worked with young people. For the moment, none of what I perceived was mentioned. After speaking with her a little more, regarding her concerns, she revealed to me of her own accord, that she was also a teacher.

After receiving permission, I entered into the Dark World and found myself on a plateau. My spirit guide pointed all around and what I saw was darkness. I asked my spirit guide what this was about, and she revealed that it was one of the places where the "dead" exist. Then I was directed by my spirit guide to the left. As we walked in that direction through the black void, a scene began to take shape. There appeared beyond the ridge of the plateau separated by water, a male image. He was in shadow and did not want to reveal himself fully. My spirit guide gave permission for me to ask who he was. He said he was Anna's father and seemed to know immediately why I had come.

To prove his existence, the father revealed the name Jim and also the name Dorothy. He then showed me a watch on his left wrist and a small gold ring on his hand which he held up for me to see, pointing to its center. I could not see the center clearly, but it looked as if it had a type of diamond chip in it. I told him I had come on behalf of Anna. He said he knew. And then before me he held out in a red dishcloth containing five pieces of Anna that he had stolen from her. As he opened the cloth further, I noticed the smile on his face. Beaming with what he thought was love, he clung to the pieces that he knew he had to give back.

At first he was reluctant, mentioning that these are things about her he loved and he really did not want to give them back. I spoke with him and said I had come on her behalf to receive them and that it was important for both of them to all Anna to claim her power. He understood that. Then, one of my other spirit guides flew over and swiftly scooped up the cloth from his grasp. It was carried to me in a net-type bag. At that point the father indicated that he desperately needed forgiveness, and at the time he took the pieces, he was not stable at all.

His desperation, uncontrollable tears and pleas for forgiveness, were sincere. He hoped Anna would do so. I asked if there was anything I could do for him. He said no, except to relay to me through a young male spirit helper who had appeared to assist him, that the only thing he needs is for Anna to forgive him. With that, a parting gesture was given to him in thanks for the return of the pieces.

My spirit guide then took me again into the Dark World, but this time there was a beautiful meadow. Large flowers of every color — bright reds, beautiful blues, verdant green plants, and the fresh scents, made my senses come alive. It was a beautiful place in the lower world, a place, my spirit guide revealed to me, where children play. I asked my spirit guide, "Is Anna here?" The answer came back, "Yes." I called out for her, and there she appeared — a little girl not more than five years of age beaming, playing. The piece of her was beautiful, creative, all that was "Oz" — the land of Oz and Jiminy Cricket, which was what she indicated to me. I came up to her and asked if this was Anna. She smiled and nodded.

I asked her if she was willing to return back to the adult Anna who needs her now. She gestured that she was and indicated to me that she wanted to be sure that Anna the adult would take care of her. I assured her that Anna would certainly try to do her best. The reason for her departure into the lower world as a very young child was not revealed in a clear cut way, but the little girl indicated to me that she felt it was best that she stay in this place until now. Willingly, the little girl came back.

All the pieces were blown into Anna. After that I was instructed to clean out the energy field around her throat and heart area which had been clogged up. This I did. Then Anna was sealed up with the use of my turtle rattle.

After welcoming her home, Anna laid there waiting for me to complete my notes of the journey. I noticed she became tense. She told me she was feeling pains in her upper chest area. I told her it will be all right, and waited. Anna rose to a sitting position pressing her hands against her chest. The pain stopped. Suddenly, she began to breathe very fully and deep — on purpose! I noticed her eyes were wide open in amazement. I questioned her. Anna looked at me and said that for the first time in her life she could breathe deeply. She was completely astonished at being able to do this. Quite frankly, I was just as amazed! I had not known, because Anna did not reveal it to me beforehand, that she had trouble breathing throughout her life.

As I revealed the journey to her and the pieces that had come back, Anna validated to me, that her father's middle name was Jim and that she did have an Aunt Dorothy. These were two of the things that had been revealed to me in the lower world. She also said that her father definitely wore a watch on his left wrist and also had a gold ring with a diamond chip in it. Further, she told me that her father had passed on in spirit.

The little girl retrieved was very much a piece that Anna said she could relate to. She also told me she really enjoyed the Wizard of Oz and Jiminy Cricket as a child. I told her that this piece would reveal more to her personally as time goes on. I asked Anna to get back in touch with me within approximately seven days, because I wanted to hear how she was doing. She agreed.

When Anna called, she was thrilled! She revealed that her energy level was better, that she was still breathing deeply, and that the aspects that brought back from her father revealed much information to her. Even in counseling, Anna was now able to have better eye contact with her therapist. She felt she was more able to express herself and that her focus was much better than before.

Anna revealed that she did a lot of crying for the first couple of days. After that, she literally "felt good, so good to be back home!" Anna said she was experiencing a deep warmth inside her that felt extremely comforting, something she had not felt for a long time. Since then (approximately a year later), Anna revealed that she is still experiencing full deep breathing, and continues to show tremendous improvement, not only in counseling, but in her personal life as well. I am so happy for her, and consider it an honor to have been of service on her behalf.

CASE # 4, by Mary Buckner, R.N.

SR/E is helping people take charge of their own healing and letting them realize what is possible. To see them grow and make positive changes is exciting work.

My own journey into this work came as a result of a New Year's resolution. I was a restless soul, seeking new direction. Do not tempt the forces that be — if the intent is sincere, Great Spirit always responds! Being in traditional nursing for many years, it seemed I was always looking for better ways to work with people. SR/E has been a process that cuts through to what needs to be healed and allows the individual to be working with and for themselves.

It is necessary that each one realize their own responsibility and make a commitment to growing. We, my guides and I, can facilitate getting parts back; but, then the ball is in your court. Exceptions do occur, as with any work, as in the example of small children and people mentally incapable of working with the energy. Those cases call for a journey to the higher self to receive permission to do the work. If permission is granted, the work can be done. When changes take place, we know that Great Spirit is still in charge.

We are feeling the need to reach for spiritual growth in these times and Great Spirit is urging us to strive for wholeness. Soul Recovery and Extraction is one of the ways people can work toward the healing of spirit.

The following story comes from a client of mine — a young woman who has been willing to work and accept the challenge! My thanks to her for her willingness to share a very personal experience. Great Spirit often works with much humor and love to manifest changes in our three dimensional world. It has been a privilege to be a part of this journey. A joyous journey indeed when we unite body, mind and spirit in balance and wholeness. This is Carol's (not her real name) personal account of her experience with soul recovery:

"It would be an understatement for me to say that soul recovery changed my life. I had it done seven months ago, shortly after my 31st birthday. I was at a point where nearly every aspect of my life was unsatisfactory. I had problems with people taking advantage of me in relationships, was recently divorced, had a job I loathed and a tyrannical boss. I had thirty pounds of extra weight I was unable to shed and continual problems with worry, anxiety and money. I seemed to make the same mistakes over and over again. In short, I was a mess and was very unhappy. I felt a terrible emptiness inside and had no idea how to begin to get my life put back together. I was under so much pressure at work that I felt I would have a nervous breakdown if something was not done soon. I did not know what I wanted or what to do. I was desperate and confused and knew I was in big trouble.

My mother heard about soul recovery from a friend and made an appointment for herself and told me about it. I had read many self-help and metaphysical books, but really had no idea what shamanism or soul recovery was. I had tried everything else so I agreed to make an appointment with Mary. She gave me some simple exercises I could do to protect myself before going to work and we set the appointment up for a couple of weeks later. As the time passed until my appointment, I began to feel very excited that something good was going to happen, although things were still very bad at work.

I was taking full time graduate study courses in the evening so I had class the night of my soul recovery. After class I went home and crawled into bed. I had some strange sensations. These feelings I can't describe well, but I sensed a change in the energy around me. The next day when I spoke to Mary she told me about my soul recovery. I was astounded that although she knew practically nothing about me, she had returned with soul parts from some of my most traumatic periods of my life. My ex-husband still had a part, and my mother had a part that she was protecting. This made sense to me because I knew my mother had been very worried about me. Mary also retrieved a wonderful mountain lion for me as a spirit guide. I was thrilled since I love all cats very much. Mary gave me some suggestions for working with the newly returned fragments and my spirit guide, and asked me to call in a week. Her work was done, but mine was only beginning.

About a day later, I contracted a head cold that was just bad enough to keep me in bed. I slept for several days straight. I tried to get in contact with my parts and my animal, but for several days I had the sense I was being "watched", yet they weren't sending me any information. On the third day, I felt compelled to get out of bed and sit down at my computer. I didn't know why I was doing this, but I began to type questions into my word processor for the fragments and my power animal. I was shocked when my fingers started to type replies. I know my head was not keeping up with the pace of the messages. It was as if my body was a conduit or a channel for their message. I mechanically did the typing, but the thoughts were not directly mine.

I came in contact with all my parts and for the next several days we discussed the events of my life that had caused them to leave and what I could do to restore harmony. They seemed relieved that I was at last paying attention to them. After these "discussions," I had a lot more clarity about my problems. I understood, for the first time in my life, why I always felt unloved and insecure. I had loving people around me, but would push them away; then, I would draw people in who were not loving, and make matters worse.

I kept detailed records of all these experiences so I could discuss them with Mary. In my experience I had had a difficult time in my twenties. Most of my missing parts were from that time span. I asked them what I could do for them and they suggested I relive my twenties. I wondered how to do this and they told me to seek joy and be aware. Later, I made three new friends, all in their twenties, who have done an excellent job (without knowing it) of bringing me into contact again with the experience of being in my twenties, except this time, it is fun and expansive, and I'm enjoying it much more than I did when I actually was that age.

Within two weeks of my soul recovery, two people who I was having a difficult time with disappeared from my life of their own accord, which gave me a great sense of relief. Others began to come in that were in far greater harmony with me. Odd "coincidences" happened that I know were a result of the work of my spirit guide on my behalf. My boss suddenly started leaving me alone; my teachers at school became good friends who I could turn to for support and for career guidance; I began to lose weight without doing anything unusual. Most importantly, I began to feel really, really good and happy — real, genuine joy. The happier I became, the better things got and that pattern continues to this day.

One day, I was discussing my relationships with men with my mountain lion and asked her to find me a more suitable mate. Several weeks later someone I barely know from school asked me out. He showed up at my house wearing a tie with a small mountain lion on it. I nearly fainted! At that moment, I knew I could relax because my mountain lion had everything under control. This has turned out to be a fun and uplifting relationship that serves all my needs perfectly at this time.

I have started to meditate, and I journey with a drumming tape to discuss things with my mountain lion. She has a warm and wonderful sense of humor and makes me see the best of all situations. She has brought other spirit guide animals to me for special purposes, and I can always call on her when I feel I need extra safety or confidence. I have found that all I need to do is be specific about what I want, or ask her to help me decide what I want, and within a couple of weeks whatever I was working on is improved. She guides me to books I need to read, people I should know and experiences that are for my higher good.

Often I see images in my head like quick snapshots, and she will be doing something to make me laugh or to make a point. I often see her dressed up in strange outfits (football jerseys, baseball caps, weskits, high top basketball shoes). I asked her about this once and she commented that one of the nice things about "sharing realities" is the ability for her to do more human things. She finds as much growth for herself as she provides to me, so the relationship is quite symbiotic.

On one of my journeys, I was surprised to discover that she had just had five cubs! I quickly called Mary to find out what this was about. I told Mary the names of the cubs and my mountain lion pointed out that I would learn something from each of them. I now journey with them frequently, and each does have a special talent or gift. It is quite remarkable that I am able to notice the differences in each of their personalities.

Another day I had journeyed to talk with my mountain lion and she suggested we run through the meadow. This is one of her favorite things to do. We run as fast as we can through golden grass and I gain the ability to feel as if I am her. I see through her eyes and feel her muscles ripple as we run. On this particular day, she took me to a place she called "Valley of the Shamans." In the Valley was a lone Indian man dancing around a campfire. I was used to seeing animals in my journeys, but not people, so I asked who he was. She told me his name, and said that I had known him since I was a child.

I suddenly remembered a time when I was three or four that I saw an Indian man in war paint and full Indian dress looking in my bedroom window. I became hysterical, and ran for my parents. My father looked all around the house, but no one was there and there were no footprints in the flower beds. I grew up in a rather affluent neighborhood and the chances of an Indian in war paint looking in windows was very slim; but I knew he was real. It took my parents several hours to calm me down.

As I stood by the fire with my mountain lion, the Indian looked up at me and said he was sorry for scaring me then, but we have much work to do together and he was a little too anxious to get started. Then, he made a joke about being nonphysical and still not having perfect judgement. He laughed loudly at his little joke and I became comfortable, yet very intrigued. He told me that I am a Shaman, too, and have been called upon to use my talents (I am twenty-five percent Cherokee, so I believe my genetic heritage has at least something to do with this). Since that day, he has been present in every journey I make and I frequently get little messages from him that pop into my mind or turn up in some serendipitous way. I am grateful that they will tirelessly answer any question I ask (even the most trivial) in a direct and humorous way. They help me see the humor in life situations which, in turn, makes my personal growth much more joyful.

Every day is a joyous adventure now. I have lost my extra weight, my career prospects are very bright, I have finished graduate school, I have friends I adore and who support me in everything I do. I have an overwhelming sense nearly every day that something wonderful will happen. I feel whole, complete, content and I worry less and trust my feelings much more. My health has also improved a great deal. It is now much easier for me to know what I want. I have greater clarity in my thinking and am able to make more discriminating choices in all aspects of my life. I am often asked what I am doing to have made these changes; people can't believe I am even the same person. Now that I have become more clear, I am of more value to others as well; and, I am able to give genuine assistance to those I come in contact with.

I trust that anything can be accomplished when I ask for assistance from my guides, and I am clear about my goals. Sometimes things don't happen exactly as I have asked, but events occur that have an even better outcome than I could imagine. I now am a firm believer in this process. It has truly changed my life. The Shaman brings back the fragments for you, but I believe your intention to work on integrating the parts and on building a relationship with your power animal is the key to putting these miracles to work for you in your daily life. When I began this seven months ago, I would never have believed what was possible; but now, very little surprises me. I believe anything is truly possible if you are willing to get clear bout what you want and then ask for help to get it.

CASE # 5, by Glenn Malec

Faith requested an SR/E after attending a seminar where the topic was introduced. Details of the session were settled over the phone. This would be a long distance journey, about two hundred miles separated us. Midnight was the agreed time that I would journey for her.

On the journey, I found a small girl who was cringing by herself, afraid that she could not accept who she was. I talked gently to her and explained that the adult Faith was quite happy with her life as a lesbian and even had a wonderful woman to share her life with. The six-year-old soul piece perked up at that and instantly wanted to return. She came back with me, wanting Faith to love her.

I was then led to a fourteen-year-old piece of Faith's soul who was encircled by her peers. They were taunting her for being different and not like them. She was lesbian and they were heterosexual. I realized that those mocking Faith caused her to lose a piece of herself. I walked up to the piece and explained that Faith has her confidence and would very much welcome the piece back. A sparkle of hope showed in her eyes. Yes, she would return, providing Faith would protect her. The fourteen-year-old piece joined hands with the six-year-old piece.

Next, I was led to the Dark World where a piece of Faith in her twenties was locked in a cage. The piece was sad. Drawing nearer to the cage, I saw a woman standing to the right of it. "This is my daughter," the woman stated. "She's going to stay there until she does what I want her to do."

Suddenly, another cage appeared to the left of the first one with another piece of Faith in her twenties as well. A man stood next to it.

"That's right. We're her parents and we know what's best for her. We want her to be normal and she'll stay right here until she is."

When these pieces of Faith saw me, they became anxious to be released from their captivity. I turned to the upset parents and told them that Faith was normal and had a healthy, loving relationship with a special woman.

"You can't change what was and is," I explained. "It's time to let Faith get on with her life and you get on with yours." I offered each of the parents a rose quartz heart adding, "This will help you to heal and to bring you the peace you seek."

Reluctantly, they opened the cages and both pieces came with me. I took them to Faith and blew them into her heart chakra and crown chakra.

The following day, Faith called and we discussed the journey in detail. Faith told me that her partner had been awake in the quiet house while the journey was ongoing. Her partner was startled to hear drumming in the bedroom as the SR took place! Once the drumming stopped, both of them went into the hall and discovered a feather lying on the floor!

I was impressed by these events, to say the least. The feather is now part of Faith's treasured items. Each piece was validated by Faith and the events surrounding their losses. These pieces have given Faith energy and a bounce in her step, which had been missing for quite some time. She has also received valued memories of her past.

CASE # 6, by Ai Gvhdi Waya

Sam was a black man in his mid-twenties, about 5'11", and overweight. He'd just gotten out of the Air Force after a four year hitch. His mother asked me to journey for him and bring back his pieces.

My chief guide took me first to the Real World, where I saw a baby, probably seven months old, crawling around on a linoleum floor in a cotton diaper. He was crawling as fast as he could go, heading toward a wall (papered with yellow wallpaper designs) and two pieces of furniture that sat against it. Sam hid between the pieces of furniture because his parents were yelling at one another. The baby was frightened by the shouting and anger; buffeted emotionally by the argument. Sam's father came over and picked him up, but Sam howled his head off. His father became angry and set Sam back down on the floor, where he quickly crawled back into his hiding place between the pieces of furniture.

I came over to Sam and asked him if he'd like to go home, to grown-up Sam. Without hesitation, the baby lifted his arms and I scooped him up off the floor and we took him home to Sam, the adult.

Next, I was sent to the Real World. I was flying across America, then over the Atlantic, and finally saw that I was in Europe. Mystified, I wondered where we were going for this piece. My hawk and I landed in a dark cellar-like bar that was dimly lit. There was singing in a foreign language that sounded like German to me. The bar was smoky, and a lot of men in civilian clothes sat around circular tables, talking with beer in hand.

I saw Sam sitting at one of the tables. A big, burly black man appeared in a dark green Army uniform — possibly a sergeant or NCO. Things suddenly went dark for me, and I felt Sam getting pushed and shoved around. I heard men grunting and cursing. There was a fight between Sam and this sergeant. The sergeant had a hunk of Sam's black hair in his hand, and I asked for it back. The sergeant eyed me angrily and didn't really want to give it back, but grudgingly, he did — but not before bad-mouthing Sam to me.

After I brought back Sam's hair, my hawk again took off and we remained in the Real World. I saw a large swimming hole coming into view. There were five or six boys of all ages running and diving off an old board into the water. Sam was nine or ten years old. He had gotten into trouble because he couldn't swim well, going under twice before finding footing to get to shore. He almost drowned — or feared he was going to drown.

I brought him back with me and placed the pieces back into the sleeping Sam. As I later wrote out my report, I began to think about the symbols I'd retrieved for Sam. The first two were self-explanatory, and I felt they'd really happened in this lifetime for Sam. The hair the sergeant had held meant that he had control over Sam — he had him by the hair of his head, so to speak.

The nearly drowning in water could have really happened, or the water might have symbolized emotional problems. Sam could have had problems at that age, and figuratively, been drowning in a lot of emotions. I recalled he had lost a piece as a baby because of family fighting. Had the fighting/dysfunctional family unit continued after that? I'd ask him the next morning when he was to call at an agreed upon time.

Sam confirmed the next morning that his mother and father had fought like cats and dogs until they divorced. Sam had no recall as a young baby, but did double-check the fighting and dysfunctional problems in his family brought on by alcoholism of both parents.

The fight with the Army NCO sergeant in Germany actually happened, Sam told me. However, it wasn't a fist fight. The way I had described the sergeant was exactly what the man had looked like, Sam confirmed. He had had to work with this sergeant who had hated him. Sam had lost a piece due to the continued stress he'd had to endure while stationed over in Germany with this NCO.

Sam couldn't recall ever drowning or coming close to drowning as a child, but he did recall a friend who almost did — he wasn't quite sure about this, and I reassured him that he'd know more abut it eventually, since that piece had returned. Also, Sam did say that at that age, his family life was an emotional roller coaster day after day, and he really did feel he was drowning in the plethora of rage/humiliation/anger that had consumed his family unit.

Since the soul repair, Sam has become more serene and not as apt to be defensive as before. He's glad to be out of the Air Force due to the prejudice against his skin color.

This journey was an "easy" one for me — there was no threat by the soul thieves, and everything was given back to

Sam without any argument. It doesn't always happen that way, and sometimes, I'm put in great personal danger (as are my facilitators). A shaman can die in the altered state, get trapped in it, and never "wake up" from the journey. This is why it's important to have spirit guides who call the shots, protect you and tell you what to do when you're in their environment.

CASE # 7, by Ai Gvhdi Waya

An Austrian client called me and asked for soul recovery and extraction. Dulcea was in her middle forties and a successful historical fiction writer in the United States — even though she lived in Austria. A linguist and translator of five languages, Dulcea had roots on both sides of the world — in Russia, where she has aristocratic lineage and here in America, where her Russian mother lived until her death.

Dulcea had been in a fifteen year marriage where he was being actively controlled and manipulated by her husband, Frederick. She had been terribly codependent for many years, but with the success of her first book, she was beginning to gain a new sense of hard-won confidence. As a result of this growth and change in Dulcea, the husband had become very overbearing. Dulcea told me she was suffocating within the marriage and could see nothing but divorce in her future. She asked if journeying might help her and Frederick. I said yes, that getting one's pieces back is always helpful — but I couldn't promise that a crumbling marriage would stay together as a result.

There are not guarantees on such things in life, however, but receiving one's pieces back, change will occur, usually within three months of getting those pieces returned. Dulcea told me she understood and was willing to take the risk in order to become whole.

I entered my altered state and asked my Indian guide if I could travel on Dulcea's behalf. I was given permission and found myself flying in the Real World with my hawk. As we entered Dulcea's house, I found her asleep in her bed.

Taking off, we continued in the Real World until we were over a large, rolling green cow pasture. I saw Dulcea, age sixteen, sitting on a tree stump wearing a simple cotton dress, weeping. As I approached her, I asked her why she was crying. Looking up, her face bathed with tears, eyes reddened, she said that Klaus, her first and only love, had stolen her heart and was gone.

I journeyed to Klaus, who was in a woodshed working. As I walked up to him, he acted as if he knew why I'd come. I told him who I was representing, and he gave me a sheepish look. From the pocket of his trousers he pulled out a heart-shaped locket and handed it to me — it was Dulcea's heart — saying he was sorry he'd stolen it.

The next place we journeyed on Dulcea's behalf was to the Real World and to her husband, Frederick. He stood there with an orange ball of light in his hands. I recognized it as Dulcea's navel chakra energy that he'd taken from her. He didn't want to give it back, hoarding it like a miser. Frederick backed away from me when I slowly approached him, repeatedly saying that if he gave the orange energy back, Dulcea would be lost to him. In tears, he begged me not to take the life-giving energy from him — it was all he'd ever had.

I gently explained that without the energy, Dulcea could not be a whole person. Is that what Frederick really wanted? Control over her, and not a real, give-and-take partnership? Shamed, Frederick hesitantly gave it back, sobbing that the marriage would be destroyed as a result. I couldn't give Frederick any assurances on way or another, but gave him a gift in return, hoping to somehow assuage his pain. Then, I took the piece back to the sleeping Dulcea.

Again, we journeyed, this time to the Dark World, where I found Dulcea slogging in a very darkened swamp. Mud was clinging to her legs, sucking her down deeper into the mire. She was struggling, but losing the battle, and the mud was slowing her progress through the swamp. Everything was very gloomy and depressing around her as we arrived. When Dulcea saw us, she stopped. Her clothing was damp and muddied; her hair tangled and dirty, with exhaustion written across her features.

Dulcea was disoriented and confused. She complained of being very tired emotionally and physically. I asked her what she was doing in the swamp, and Dulcea looked around and said she wasn't sure about her life or where it was going. Everything, she said, was in a state of confusion. The decision to stay or leave Frederick tore at her. I asked Dulcea if she wanted to return home, and she held out her' arms to me and we took her out of that depressing swamp.

Returning to the bedroom, I gave the pieces back to Dulcea and left. The next morning, as planned, Dulcea called me from Austria and I told her about the journey. She verified that a young man, whose name was very close to "Klaus" had indeed, stolen her heart — and that he was German — she, Austrian. Secondly, upon waking that morning, she felt much more vital, and filled with hope. I told her about giving back her navel chakra energy, and the fact that she felt stronger and more confident was my double-check that this piece was, indeed, reintegrating.

I told her that when navel chakra energy is stolen or lost, codependence will take root in the person. Frederick had constantly manipulated her through guilt and other psychological and emotional tactics to give, give, give to him — at her expense. Dulcea had spent fifteen years giving herself to the point of having nothing left for herself — a very common codependent condition. Now, with the return of the navel chakra energy, I counseled her to begin to shift to becoming a receiver.

Dulcea understood clearly what that meant — making time for herself, giving herself not only a hiatus, but gifts that were invigorating and energizing to herself instead of always giving them away to needy Frederick.

The third piece found in the swamp, she said, happened six months earlier in her life. She felt completely depressed, unable to make any decisions about the marriage or her husband. I told her with the return of these pieces, that she would start seeing the situation more clearly than before —

and therefore, be able to make more reliable decisions about the present and her future — with or without Frederick.

A year has passed since that journey on Dulcea's behalf. Frederick also requested SR/E. By receiving her pieces back, Dulcea has clearly seen how she has contributed to the crippled marriage, and has made the decision to no longer be codependent.

She has identified her past patterns of reaction or action with Frederick, and instituted new, more positive responses to the marriage. This has strained their relationship greatly. Unfortunately, Frederick flipped off his pieces that were recovered for him, and in the end, he became greedy and needy for Dulcea all over again. Dulcea has now asked for a divorce from him, has gone on to sell two more historical novels and is continuing to grow and integrate.

CASE # 8, by Gary Gent

I have many clients overseas, with a number of them in Israel. One particular case that shocked even me about the positive use of extraction, follows. This is not to say that every time we do an extraction, that miracles happen, but in this case, they did, and I'd like to share it with you.

Judith was in her sixties, and lives in Jerusalem. Her granddaughter, Ruth, had called me on her behalf. Ruth begged me to make a journey for Judith because in two weeks, she was due to go into the hospital for surgery to remove a malignant cancer tumor in her pancreas. Judith also was diagnosed with Parkinson's Disease.

After receiving permission, the first place my chief guide took me was in the Real World. I saw Judith, at age seven, and she was being beaten with a whip by her father. The impression I received from the scene I saw was that the father was teaching Judith obedience. I stopped the beating and asked Judith if she'd like to return home. Tearfully, she said she would.

The next place we were sent was the Real World. I found a sleeveless blouse that belonged to Judith. The age impression was twenty-seven years old, and the blouse had a v-neck. The material was linen and had a star on it. I was told this blouse dealt with religion and marriage issues for Judith.

The rest of the journey for Judith was comprised of extraction. In the brain and lower, portion, near the occiput, there was a dark area. When I see this, I know that the area is not functioning normally. My guide directed a violet and yellow ray of color to fill the darkened area. Then, we entered the dark area. The brain matter was filled with brown, crystal-like objects. The effects of the violet and yellow rays were to dislodge the crystal-like objects and I began to scoop them up and out of the area. This process continued until all the crystal-like objects were removed from the darkened region. My chief guide then filled thousands of nerve endings and synapse regions with white light.

Next, my chief guide showed me Judith's heart and there was a lot of sludge-like material in and around the chakra propellers themselves. I cleaned these out so that her chakra could once again, begin to turn and process the prana or energy that is all around us and that keeps us healthy.

The last place we worked was Judith's pancreas. I saw the tumor, which was quite large, and located on the upper right quadrant of the endocrine gland. I removed the tumor and filled the void with healing green light.

Judith confirmed that her parents were very strict, and that she had been beaten a number of times as a youngster, to be shown obedience. The blouse meant a great deal to her, as they were very religiously inclined, and she'd been married for over forty years.

A week after the journey, and unknown to me at the time, Judith was scheduled to go to the hospital in Jerusalem to get the last round of tests before she went into surgery the following week. I received an excited call from Ruth, who was bubbling over with joy. When the tests had been done on the pancreas, the tumor was no longer in evidence! It was completely GONE. Further, Judith's doctors have film showing the tumor previously, and it had been growing, so in their minds, there was no way the tumor could have disappeared just like that.

But it had. Needless to say, Judith was overjoyed, and she didn't have to have the surgery after all. However, she still has the shaking and trembling connected with Parkinson's Disease, and that has not diminished hardly at all.

I can't explain why the tumor was taken, but the Parkinson's wasn't helped. As a facilitator, I just do as I'm directed in the altered state. It has only been three months since the extraction work concerning her brain and nerve endings, and it could be that Judith will need more pieces returned and then more work done on the brain, afterward. Many times, especially in chronic disease conditions, all or most of the pieces need to be returned first before we see progress or a slowing down of the disease. Then, extraction can be done, and it will generally help.

Case # 9, by Gary Gent

I was contacted in July of 1993 by a friend in Southern California concerning Julie, who had been helped all she could be by allopathic medicine. Julie was twenty-eight years old and had been diagnosed with Leukemia for many years. On the date I was contacted by this friend, Julie was in the hospital, on life support equipment. Her white blood cell count was under 3,000 and there was massive infection in the abdomen that was not responding to antibiotics. I was informed by my friend that the doctors had told Julie's family there was nothing else to be done and they disconnected the life support system.

My friend asked me if I could journey for Julie, even though Julie was unconscious and unable to give verbal permission. I said yes, providing that either my chief guide or Julie's gave me permission to undertake a journey in her behalf, and the friend said that was more than fair. I could contact Julie in the altered state and talk to her directly or with her chief guide, since this is what we normally do when someone is in a coma, unconscious or drugged so heavily that they aren't conscious.

I scheduled the journey for the next day since it was a life-and-death emergency. On July 4th, I entered the journey on Julie's behalf. I received permission and traveled to Julie with my guides. On entering Julie's hospital room, I saw two light beings in the room, about half way to her bed.

Light beings, or angels, are always in the room of someone who is in the process of dying. The closer they are to the bed where the dying person is lying, the closer they are to leaving this earth plane. I talked to the light beings, informed them of my mission and asked if they could assist her into the light, to die. The light beings informed me that she would die in three days if nothing was done for Julie, and that yes, they would assist her into the light after she died. I thanked the light beings and turned my attention to Julie. I went to her bed where she met me.

Although she was physically unconscious, I was able to talk to her spirit, which was completely conscious, lively and animated. We talked at length, discussing her situation and what myself and my guides could do for her. Julie decided that I would be allowed to journey in her behalf.

The first thing that we did was performed an extraction on Julie. She was placed in an "altered state intensive care unit," and the massive infection in her abdomen was removed. The infection was caused by a previous surgery in which an object, part of sponge, was left inside Julie. In the altered state the infection appeared as a sickly greenish mass that infused her body on several levels.

After removal of the infection, a black tar-like gooey mass was visible in her solar plexus area which was also removed. I was then directed to flush her body with white light to remove the last vestiges of the infection. My attention was then directed to an object in her solar plexus. The object, glowing a radioactive green color, was shaped like two triangles joined at the points. We removed the object.

With the infection removed, we then turned our attention to the low white blood count (leukemia). We applied healing gold light to Julie's skeletal structure and simultaneously infused her bone marrow with white, healing light. Next, we applied silver healing light to Julie's glandular system, to strengthen and heal her body's defenses. Finally, we processed Julie through the soul filter for removal of contamination that was too small for me to see.

I asked my guides if this was all that could be done. I was told that soul pieces needed to be returned and retrieved. Julie game me three pieces she had of other people in her possession. These were returned. A man also had two pieces of Julie that belonged in Julie's heart chakra. He was keeping Julie's heart pieces in a trophy case for display.

At the end of the journey, I asked the light beings what effect this would have on Julie. Would she still be taken to the light? They told me that Julie now had 21 days in which to make her decision — a decision to live or die. The light beings were simply loving guardians (we all have them) who always assist us in many, every day ways and especially, when we're ready to die. It was not their decision to make to take Julie into the light — it was HER decision.

At this point in Julie's case, I'll explain some extenuating circumstances in this case. Julie's family is very religious and would scoff at the whole idea of SR/E as being helpful. As a result, the family is, to this day, unaware of this journey being undertaken — thanks to a friend.

One week after I completed the journey, Julie's infection decreased seventy-five percent, and the white blood count had increased from 3,000 to 30,000! Quite a remarkable change. A count of 30,000 is high, and considered good for a leukemia patient recovering from a bout with low blood count. Needless to say, the doctors attending Julie were baffled by the dramatic turn around, especially since they removed her life support systems to allow her to die with dignity.

One month after the journey, Julie's health has improved to the point where she's been discharged from the hospital and returned home to continue her life.

THE BENEFITS OF SOUL
RECOVERY AND EXTRACTION

The benefits of soul recovery and extraction are so incredibly powerful that this healing tool makes everything else pale in comparison; indeed, it makes every other healing tool a secondary action.

Soul recovery and extraction can cut years off therapy, help any illness whether of spiritual, mental, emotional or physical origin, and enable the person in harmony and balance.

HOW OFTEN SHOULD SOUL
RECOVERY BE DONE?

Once a year after the initial SR/E, the client should ask their shaman to take a "maintenance" journey (January is a good month — new year, new beginning) and see if SR/E is needed.

Other times you may want to consider SR/E which could include:

- *If you suffer a traumatic shock (on any level; you should ask your shaman to journey to check out the situation and see if SR or E is needed.*
- *If you feel, sense or have a gut feeling that a person in your life has "latched" onto a piece of you, is obsessing over you in some way and cannot release you, call your facilitator.*
- *If you suddenly have a drop in energy that does not right itself within twenty four hours, contact your facilitator. This may indicate that someone has plugged into your aura and is sucking your vital force or energy from you for their own use.*
- *If any of the symptoms covered in Chapter 1 return, call your facilitator immediately.*

DID YOU KNOW:

1. SR/E can be performed on animals just as easily as it can on humans. Indeed, it can be performed on plants, properties, homes or any "child" of Mother Earth — it is not necessarily limited to a human being! If your house isn't selling, call your facilitator.

2. SR/E should be performed by every able-bodied shaman to return to Mother Earth pieces that were stolen by human beings. Further, her etheric body is deteriorating daily (the "holes" over the polar caps) and shamans should, in their spare time, direct their extraction and healing energies to helping repair these holes.

3. Extraction greatly helps people who have such ailments as sinus infection, sinusitis or infection in the root of a tooth. Recently, I had Mary Buckner journey for me because I had a molar that was infected and the dentist pronounced root canal! I called Mary to see if she would journey, if possible, to extract whatever infection was in my tooth and jaw area and get it out of there. She did, and my tooth is no longer infected — voila! No root canal!

Extraction can be performed on anything in the human, animal, organic or inorganic realm. For example, I journeyed the night before to help my sister, Nancy, who had to have surgery performed on her left knee. She had injured it a year before, and the leading sports surgeon in Seattle only gave her a 40% chance of recovery. I extracted (with the approval and assistance of her chief guide) a lot of blockage in both knees, plus worked with the torn ligament that would be repaired the next morning by the surgeon. The good news is that she now has 100% use of her knee!

CHAPTER 4

INTEGRATING YOUR RETURNED SOUL PIECES

I always tell clients to do several things in regards to the pieces brought back to them:

1. Welcome each piece home (and sincerely mean it) the first 24 hours after the journey.
2. Ask each piece for the next twenty-eight days, once a day:
     a) What gift or knowledge did you bring back to me?
     b) What can I do to make you want to stay?
3. Tell each piece: How much you love them, that you are glad they are back and that you want them to stay. Do this for one full month after the recovery.

Sometimes the return of a piece is very traumatic, and a therapist needs to be in place to help the person deal with the re-integration of that piece. I sometimes utilize homeopathy or Bach Flower remedies at this point with my clients to get them up and over this period more quickly and with less pain. These are extreme cases, and ninety percent of my clients do not need either of the above. All the facilitators are knowledgeable about homeopathy and Bach Flower remedies, should you need them.

When I know that sexual molestation has taken place, I urge the client to read *The Courage to Heal* and tell them to stay in touch with me should the memories of the trauma come flooding back to them. Eventually, within 3 to 12 months, they will return. I also tell the client to have a therapist they have chosen (hopefully a woman with rape/molestation counseling background) in place should the dam break on this dark, trauma-ridden part of her life.

Everyone integrates pieces differently — there's no specific time here because all people are individuals, and their healing process is their own. In general, within 72 hours of a recovery, some clients knows it happened. In fifty percent of the cases a person may feel little or nothing in regards to the healing that has taken place. Often, the return is so subtle that the client will swear there has been no change. However, three months after the journey, they will be able to look back and realize that they have changed in many ways. The healing process is different for everyone. Within three months, if all has gone according to plan, the pieces are completely integrated and fully functioning within the person once again.

Within twenty-four hours of your SR/E being performed for you, you will be asked to call your shamanic facilitator at a specific time so they can give you a report on what pieces and/or extraction work was done. Some facilitators, such as Gary Gent and Mary Buckner, have fax machines, and this is especially helpful in contacting overseas clients. At this time, your facilitator will also give you the following instructions in order to help you with the integration of your pieces:

1.   After receiving your verbal report from your facilitator and when you have a quiet, uninterrupted moment, welcome each of your pieces home, telling them how happy you are that they have returned and that you love them very much. Visualize each piece as it was returned to you, and recall the circumstances surrounding it. Some clients throw a party to welcome home their pieces. Others go on vacation to be alone, contemplate or meditate with their newly recovered pieces. Still others buy a gift for their lost childhood pieces now returned. There are two questions you must ask each piece, asking:

(a)   What gift or knowledge did you bring back for me?

(b)   What can I do to make you want to stay with me?

2.   Do not expect an answer immediately — although that can happen in some cases. Usually, it may be anywhere between three weeks to three months before you know what the gift is. So, be patient and gracefully receive whatever the gift is. It is always good! Whenever a piece is brought back, it inevitably brings something of value back to you — whether it be memories of a "blank spot" in your life, feelings/emotions, a skill or talent, and/or a body of information you did not have before.

There will be a feeling or sense of what you must do to show this piece that you care enough to make some changes in your life to make it comfortable for it to stay. As an example, one piece I brought back for a client was a little boy at the age of six. When the client asked those questions that night, the strong impression he received was to go for a walk in the woods or out in nature. He decided that on a weekly basis, he would take time out of his type A business schedule and begin hiking in the nearby Great Smoky Mountains. Not only did the piece stay, but the client was able to recapture a wonderful part of his youth which he had previously thought was impossible to recapture and incorporate into his present lifestyle.

Another example was a woman in whose little girl piece of five years old impressed upon her in a dream some weeks after "coming home" to her that she wanted a teddy bear. The next day, while shopping, she bought one and it now stays on her bed — and the piece stayed.

3. In order to reassure each piece, you must be sincere and come from the heart the best you know how; also praise each piece. Treat each piece as if it were a well-loved child returning home to you after a very long absence. Sometimes a person has had so many pieces missing that they can no longer feel their heart of emotions and feelings. Do not worry. Just visualize and say the words — being sincere when you say them — to each piece. It is the best you can do at the time and it will be sufficient to keep the pieces with

you. Little by little, your feelings will return over a year's time, generally speaking.

The easy part is bringing the pieces home for you. The real work begins when you start the integration process as outlined above. And that's as it should be! You are responsible for yourself in all phases of your life.

I once had a client whose piece asked her to go to a child's playground to play. At first, she was hesitant; she finally trusted her own knowing on this and did it. She played on the swing, the teeter totter and merry-go-round — she had an absolute ball! So, without fail, to satisfy this piece of herself, she goes to the playground at least once a month — and has never regretted it. She comes away from the "play time" feeling good, positive, uplifted and very happy.

Another suggestion, if you choose, is to keep a journal over the first 28-day period that you go through the integration process. You may have dreams, interesting meditations, synchronistic events occur in your life, or other phenomena. After putting down your impressions, observations, feelings, dreams or other items, you can look back on this journal and see an actual pattern emerging — a new one. It can mirror the new blueprint for your life — a far more positive one, a more fulfilling and happy one.

If a piece flips off, what do I do?

Usually, once your pieces are returned, you will know for sure when a piece "flips off" or leaves you to return to the place where it was originally found. Call your facilitator and tell them what you think happened. The first thing you need to look at is whether or not you were doing all that you could integration-wise to keep the piece. Whatever the reason was for it to flip off, the facilitator will journey to find out (a) if the piece did leave you, (b) talk to the piece if it has left and find out why it left, and (c) ask if the piece will come back.

We do not force a piece to return. However, we are the best used car sales people in non-physical realms and we are pretty good at coaxing a piece into returning to you in most instances. If the piece absolutely refuses to come back, then the facilitator will journey three months later, go revisit the piece, and see if they can get it to return to you at that time. Usually, they will come home. It is a question of time.

What if the healing method does not work for you?

There are cases where a person may be consciously ready to be healed, but due to a karmic situation beyond their knowing, the SR/E may not work. Pieces may flip off, because the client is subconsciously not ready to heal. The facilitator may, at their discretion, journey to check out the situation and TRY to find out the reason why the pieces flipped off. Many times, the answer we receive is that the client is not ready to heal because they are still actively working on a karmic situation in their life. There is nothing further that a facilitator can do at this point. Normally, we ask the client to call us in three to six months and we will again journey to find out if the client is subconsciously, as well as consciously, ready to begin the healing process.

The client should never feel guilty or bad if this situation develops. But rather, to use this new information in a new and positive way to help them continue to grow. There are always times in our lives where we think we are ready to make a change, or to heal, and we aren't. In other words, we sometimes get the cart before the horse.

CHAPTER 5

SPIRIT GUIDES: LONG-TERM PROTECTION FOR A CLIENT

Another service a shamanic facilitator can render for the client is retrieving a guide, be it an animal, reptile or insect spirit guide from where they live in the Dark World. One particular case comes to mind that will beautifully illustrate this point.

A little boy, five years old (we'll call him Bobby), was a client of my facilitator, Mary Buckner. He had a long history of illness since birth, and his mother was divorced from his father. Mary had journeyed and brought back the following pieces:

1. During the birthing there was great trauma, and he lost a piece; that piece went back to the Light World.

2. His father had a huge piece of the child in the Real World.

3. His grandmother, a domineering old woman, had a piece of him in the Real World.

Further, Mary saw that each time Bobby had to visit his father for a month each year, the father and grandmother were taking even more pieces from him. Bobby did not want to visit them, he's afraid of them and cries constantly that he wants to remain home with his mother. However, she is required by law to release him to his father for a month each summer.

I talked with Mary about this and told her to ask Bobby's chief guide if we could bring up from the Dark World an animal spirit guide who would protect him from further theft by his father and grandmother.

Mary journeyed and went to the Dark World and retrieved a wolf for Bobby. The animal gave Mary his name, and she, in turn, told the mother, who informed Bobby. Normally, we never share the name of a spirit guide with anyone because it is possible another person will use or abuse the use of the guide without the other person's knowledge. In this case, the name was safe with the mother.

Mary also performed "long distance" extraction (see Chapter One) and removed blocks from his throat, sinus, lungs, chest wall and from the solar plexus area. This child had a long history of asthma, bronchitis, pneumonia and colds which always settled in the lungs.

The mother, who strongly believes in metaphysics, told Bobby what had happened, and that he had a new "playmate" — the wolf. She gave Bobby the name of his invisible friend, and he happily accepted this buddy.

The next day, the mother and son were out shopping, and Bobby saw a stuffed toy animal in a store window, which he excitedly pointed to and said that this was his new, invisible friend! Wisely, the mother bought Bobby the stuffed toy wolf. Bobby now sleeps with the wolf each night and carries it around with him during the day.

In the invisible realm, the wolf spirit guide is at Bobby's side 24 hours a day. When Bobby has to go visit his father and grandmother, he will have the wolf spirit guide who will ensure no one will take any more pieces from him.

A spirit guide acts as many things for a person: teacher, guide and protector. Spirit guides take on a suitable and acceptable form in which a person will be comfortable. For instance, someone who was a devoted Christian would probably see an angel. As for me, with my Native American heritage, I prefer to see animals. Spirit guides are light energy forms and can assume a shape or persona that is easiest for you to communicate and feel comfortable with. Spirit guides will defend their human being, and can inflict great damage upon the attacker.

They may make a frightening, audible sound as a panther spirit guide did for her human counterpart: the woman was at home late at night when a burglar tried to enter the house. She instantly asked her panther to protect her. Hiding in her hall closet, she heard this loud, aggressive growl of a huge cat emanating from the area of the door where the burglar was trying to get in. In moments she heard the burglar yelp and run off. She called the police. After their arrival and their usual questions, she went outside with them. One of the policeman pointed out to her that her very dusty and dirty car had huge paw prints that started from the hood and went to the trunk of her car. Stunned, she realized that her panther spirit guide had chased the burglar away, and left its tracks on her car to prove it!

Spirit guides will never kill a person, but they can make life miserable for them in uncounted ways that would simply take too much room to elaborate upon. Suffice to say, spirit guides, even though they are invisible, carry a great deal of energy and power. On occasion, they can even materialize in order to scare off a potential attacker or someone who would harm their human. They have been known to put puncture wounds, bites or scratches on people's arms and legs. Most often they will send word to the attacker's subconscious to leave — right now. And most of the time that suggestion alone is enough.

Spirit guides also often act as a "buffer" between the person and the potential soul thief who may unconsciously want to steal from you because they are needy in some way.

A shaman will bring a spirit guide to the person, if allowed. They will teach the person how to work with and deal with the spirit guide on a continuing basis. Then, they are left to work and educate one another from that day forward. Spirit guides are the "seeing eye dogs" of the invisible, non-physical realms that are here to help us, protect us and teach us.

In some cases of SR/E the chief guide of the person directs a facilitator to go to the Dark World and retrieve a spirit guide who can teach and protect the client. The facilitator then acts as an intermediary between the client and their chief spirit guide to accomplish this.

If you are constantly being taken advantage of, abused

in any way, taken for granted or pulled in a hundred different directions, you may need a spirit guide. This entity will give you the strength to resist, to say "no" and mean it, and regain the power to direct your own life. A facilitator can retrieve a spirit guide for you (provided the your chief guide approves).

One of the greatest gifts a shaman experiences is when he or she sees a client gain the courage to ask for soul recovery and extraction, and to watch them go through the process and become whole once more. You can save years of therapy by utilizing this amazing and almost magical process. It saves years of feeling half a person in a sense, or feeling horribly vulnerable and not knowing how to protect oneself from the hurts of the world.

Children are particularly vulnerable because they are little people without any defenders, especially when in the midst of a dysfunctional family situation. A spirit guide retrieved especially for the child will help them keep confidence and self esteem intact, as well as protect them from physical, mental and/or emotional abuse.

Usually, the acquiring of a spirit guide is a specific, single journey and is rarely combined with any SR/E journey. However, in some instances, a spirit guide will be brought back for you to work with, along with the return of missing pieces and/or an extraction. Your spirit guide is your teacher, your protector and your support. Your facilitator will counsel you over the phone on the exact technique of working with your spirit guide, which is similar to welcoming home a soul piece from the standpoint of talking to it, listening to its guidance, telling it that you love it and want its help and guidance. A spirit guide that is ignored will leave, which defeats the whole purpose in the first place. However, specific instructions will be given to you on how to work with your Spirit Guide should you receive one.

FACILITATORS WHO PERFORM SR/E who have
been chosen and trained by Ai Gvhdi Waya:

NOTE: To have soul recovery and extraction performed on your behalf, you must first read this book and educate yourself fully regarding the technique, the facilitator's responsibilities, and your responsibilities. You may order the book via the facilitator of your choice, or directly through Blue Turtle Publishing. Healing is a matter of education and Ai Gvhdi Waya has asked that those who are drawn to this method first understand it.

After reading the book, send a letter to the facilitator of your choice and ask for their comprehensive brochure. Add your phone number if you choose and they will call you collect; or they will contact you by mail. Each facilitator has a brochure with a comprehensive informational biography and a list of services available, as well as a price structure for those services. Please enclose a self-addressed and stamped envelope.

Remember: SR/E can be performed LONG DISTANCE, so it is not a matter of choosing the facilitator closest to you. Some facilitators will allow you to come to their home for the SR/E to be performed. Others will come to your area, provided a workshop has been set up, and will stay until all is accomplished for those who want SR/E performed. Some will give workshops on SR/E, what it is and its benefits. NONE of the facilitators are authorized to teach the actual SR/E method. This is decided by Ai Gvhdi Waya, alone. All facilitators can do long-distance SR/E and all have a world-wide clientele. Ai Gvhdi Waya is NOT available for SR/E.

Rosemarie Brown, MSW, Homeopathic Medicine degree (UK), medical astrologer. P.O. Box 1322, Cottonwood, AZ 86326. Fax: (520) 646-9321. E-mail: cyberdoc@sedona.net.

Mary Buckner, RN, medical astrologer. P.O. Box 670, Kingston, OK 73439. E-mail: soulbear@juno.com.

Gail Carswell, astrologer, medical astrologer, numerologist, Blue Turtle Natural Essence consultant and distributor. British Institute of Homeopathy (degree in progress). P.O. Box 1090, Cottonwood, AZ 86236. Phone/fax: (520) 634-

5211. E-mail: rockdoc@sedona.net. Available Sept. 1998.

Karen David, spiritualist medium, numerologist, author, counselor. P.O. Box 39216. Cleveland, OH 44139.

Alison Deming, MS, clinical member of marriage and family therapist. Certified sex therapist and educator. P.O. Box 1525, Camp Verde, AZ 8632.

Darcy Deming, BA, Equestrian/Biology, freelance writer, equine therapist for horse and rider. P.O. Box 1525, Camp Verde, AZ 86322. E-mail: demverde@verdenet.com.

Gail Derin, graduate of the Hahnemann Homeopathic College and Doctor of Oriental Medicine. P.O. Box 697, Cottonwood, AZ 86326. E-mail: gail@sedona.net.

Karen Durand-Meredith, licensed massage therapist, cranial-sacral therapy. P.O. Box 303, Prospect, OR 97356. E-mail: 72270.1561@CompuServe.com.

Michael J. Foltz, holistic astrologer, medical astrologer, numerologist, Blue Turtle Natural Essence consultant and distributor. British Institute of Homeopathy (in process). P.O. Box 1090, Cottonwood, AZ 86236. Phone/fax: (520) 634-5211. E-mail: Solardoc@sedona.net. Available Sept. 1998.

Gary Gent, brother of Ai Gvhdi Waya. Phone: (602) 439-5843. Fax: (602) 938-7647. E-mail: ggent@worldnet.att.net. Phoenix, AZ

Nina Gettler, lay homeopath, author. P.O. Box 60133, Seattle, WA 98160-0133. Phone/fax: (206) 368-7355. E-mail: ninaget@aol.com.

Eileen Lunderman, Lakota. Pathways, P.O. Box 501, Mission, SD 57555.

Caroline Mardon, MA (candidate), holistic experiential psychotherapist, kundalini yoga, women's rituals. 789 Carlaw Ave, #5. Toronto, ON, Canada M4K 3L2. Phone: (416) 469-5314. E-mail: hep@interlog.com. Fax: (416) 469-4605. Available September 1998.

Glenn Malec, UFO/alien specialist, astrologist. P.O. Box 186, Wildwood NJ 08260.

Jim McNamara, MBBS, ND, spiritual psychotherapist, holistic healer. 45A Simpson Ave., Toronto, ON, Canada M4K 1A1. Phone: (416) 469-5155. Fax: (416) 469-4605. E-mail: hep@interlog.com. Available September 1998.

Berenice Sara Romero, astrologer, Reiki master, degree in Homeopathic Medicine (UK), massage, healing. P.O. Box 1888, Cottonwood, AZ 86326.

Patty Running, Santee Lakota, sweat lodge leader. Route 2, Box 27, Nibrara, NB 68760.

C. Michael Smith, Ph.D., licensed psychologist, author, editor of Shamanic Applications Review. P.O. Box 0314, Niles, MI 49120. Phone: (616) 683-8972. Fax: (616) 683-0449. E-mail: ShamanicAR@aol.com.

Marvin Surkin, Ph., D., D. AC. (NCCAOM), acupuncture, Chinese herbology, psychoenergetic therapy. 3245 SW Shoals Ferry Road, Portland, OR 97221. Phone: (503) 296-7994. Fax: (503) 296-8499. E-mail: msurkin@aol,com. Available September 1998.

Coletta Swalley, Lakota. Pathways, P.O. Box 501, Mission, SD 57555.

Penny Winestock, M.Sc., psychotherapist, couple therapist, soul healer. 55 Rainsford Road, Toronto, ON, Canada M4L 3N7. Phone: (416) 693-4203. Fax: (416) 693-1069. E-mail: winestock@sympatico.ca. Available September 1998.

Grace Verte, Rev., MA, lifepath astrologer, Bach Flower Remedies consultant. P.O. Box 4272, Sedona, AZ 86340. Phone: (520) 282-4922.

To subscribe to Shamanic Applications Review magazine, published quarterly, $35/year U.S., $41/year Canada and Mexico, $47/year all other countries (U.S. funds). SAR, P.O. Box 0314, Niles, MI 49120.

PUBLISHED BY BLUE TURTLE PUBLISHING:
Soul Recovery and Extraction
    by Ai Gvhdi Waya (Eileen Nauman) $9.95
Colored Stones and Their Meaning
    by Eileen Nauman and Ruth Gent $4.95
Medical Astrology
    by Eileen Nauman $29.95

Internet web site: www.medicinegarden.com

PUBLISHED BY LIGHT TECHNOLOGY PUBLISHING:
Poisons That Heal
    by Eileen Nauman $14.95

To order, write, call or Email:
Blue Turtle Publishing
P.O. Box 2513, Cottonwood, AZ 86326
Phone/fax: (520) 634-9298
Email: docbones@sedona.net

If you would like more copies of this or any other book we publish, write us with your order and enclose a check made out to Blue Turtle Publishing. Add $1.65 per book for postage, except for *Medical Astrology*: add $4 per book. **FREE** catalog upon request. **Bookstores:** write or call for wholesale discount information.